THE *PEKING* BATTLES CAPE HORN

A true account of a voyage around Cape Horn in the bark Peking *in 1929-30; with a Foreword by Peter Stanford, President of the National Maritime Historical Society, Introduction by Electa Johnson, Afterword by Captain Johnson, commentary by Charles Brodhead, and an Appendix by Norman Brouwer, Ship Historian of South Street Seaport Museum, on the life and rebirth of the* Peking

By Captain Irving Johnson

with photographs by the author
and drawings by J.A. Wilson

SEA HISTORY PRESS

National Maritime Historical Society
Peekskill, New York

The original edition of this book was published in 1932 by Milton Bradley Company, Springfield, Massachusetts, with two additional chapters on land travels and a steamer trip home not included in this edition. The Foreword, Afterword and Appendix appeared in a reprint edition published by Sea History Press in 1977. The Appendix is adapted with permission from an article that originally appeared in the *South Street Reporter*, then the quarterly journal of the South Street Seaport Museum in New York City. The postscript to the Foreword, the Introduction by Electa (Exy) Johnson, and the commentary by Charles Brodhead have not appeared in print before.

Copyright for this book was generously donated to the National Maritime Historical Society by Captain Irving Johnson, the proceeds of book sales and any subsidiary rights to be devoted to the preservation of such historic ships as the *Peking* and to the advancement of learning in our heritage in sail.

CONTENTS

BOOKS BY IRVING JOHNSON

Round the Horn in a Square Rigger, pub. by Milton Bradley 1932
Shamrock V's Wild Voyage Home, pub. by Milton Bradley, 1933

BOOKS BY IRVING AND ELECTA JOHNSON

Westward Bound in the Schooner Yankee,
    pub. by W.W. Norton, 1936
Sailing to See, pub by W. W. Norton, 1939
Yankee's Wander World, pub. by W. W. Norton, 1949
Yankee Sails across Europe, pub. by W. W. Norton, 1962
Yankee Sails the Nile, pub. W. W. Norton, 1966

BY IRVING AND ELECTA JOHNSON AND LYDIA EDES

Yankee's People and Places, pub. by W. W. Norton, 1955

PHOTOGRAPHS

PATRONS

Publication of this new augmented edition is made possible by the generous contributions of the patrons shown below.

THE FAMILY OF JACK R. ARON

THE FURTHERMORE PROGRAM, J.M. KAPLAN FUND

WALTER J. HANDELMAN, ESQ.

MOBIL OIL CORPORATION

DOUGLAS & JEANNIE MUSTER

CAPT. & MRS. RALPH M. PACKER, JR.

S.H. & HELEN R. SCHEUER FAMILY FOUNDATION

HOWARD & SHEILA SLOTNICK

BAILEY SMITH

ALIX THORNE

ANNA GLEN VIETOR

EDWARD G. ZELINSKY

FOREWORD

CAPTAIN IRVING JOHNSON AND THE *PEKING*

On the last Friday in November 1929 the big four-masted bark *Peking* put to sea. She came down the Elbe and walked into a succession of furious, icy gales in the North Sea, barely avoiding being driven ashore. She weathered that, and then encountering head winds and dirty weather in the English Channel, had to run back to the North Sea again to get sea room. There she met a "first-class hurricane," the worst blow recorded in half a century. With that under her belt, she worked her way down the North and South Atlantic, around Cape Horn at the tip of South America, where she smashed through two "rip-snorters," for which that desolate, storm-wracked region is infamous, and so came into Talcahuano in Chile after 93 days at sea.

In her crew were two young men, Irving Johnson and his friend Charlie Brodhead, who had just graduated from Princeton University the previous spring. They shared, as Captain Johnson explains in this narrative of the voyage, "a hankering to make a voyage in one of the old-time square riggers."

Peking is, Captain Johnson notes, a "great big wagon." The ship is on exhibition to the public at the South Street Seaport Museum in New York today, where you may marvel at the ultimate in the ocean-going square-rigged sailing ship. (An appendix to this book gives some of her earlier and subsequent history.)

i

With masts seventeen stories high, she spread over an acre of canvas in thirty-two sails.

Seventy-four souls sailed in her, in all. Besides Irving and Charlie, there were the Captain, four mates, five regular sailors and fifty-four cadets, learning their seafaring the hard way as their forefathers had. There was a boatswain (senior sailorman aboard) and the seven "idlers," who stood no regular watches but worked hard to keep the crew fed and the huge structure of the ship, her sails, gear and rigging working: two cooks, steward, sailmaker, carpenter, blacksmith and radioman.

As he joined the ship, Irving Johnson saw the gear of a man lost the previous voyage brought ashore— pitiful remnants of a man's life. This was no one's fault. As Captain Johnson makes clear in his narrative written at the time, the ship was superbly well sailed.

"That is what life on a sailing ship teaches," says Captain Johnson. "Work the ship while there is life left in your body."

* * * * *

Leaving the *Peking* on the west coast of South America, Irving and his friend Charlie crossed the Andes to Argentina, from where they worked their way home aboard a British coal-burning freighter, arriving in New York in April. Johnson returned to his summer job skippering the yacht *Charmian* in New England waters. At the end of the summer of 1930, while he was laying up the boat, a friend asked him: "What are you going to do this winter?"

"Oh, some foolish thing, I suppose," he responded. His friend then asked him to come along with him on the return voyage to England of the British J-boat *Shamrock V*, which had been defeated by the *Enterprise* in that summer's America's Cup Races. The crossing was made through the center of a hurricane that made big Atlantic liners heave to in order to reduce damage from the sea. *Shamrock*'s wild voyage home (as Captain Johnson justly called it in a book by that title) was made in the fast time of eighteen days. But the real race was to see which land she would reach first—England or the floor of the Atlantic Ocean.

Captain Johnson, now showing some appreciation for *terra firma*, wandered through Europe and then worked his way home across the Atlantic on the British liner *Olympic*. The next summer he was off in the schooner *Wander Bird* under Captain Warwick Tompkins for a voyage in company with a transatlantic race, followed by extensive cruising in Europe and the West Indies and so back to Boston. On board *Wander Bird* he met Exy, who became his wife. She is a person who shares his penchant for sitting on a yard high aloft on a sailing ship and gazing at far horizons.

Only where they looked, these two went on to *sail*. In 1933 they acquired their own schooner, *Yankee*, and in this vessel and two later *Yankees* they began world cruising in which, eventually, they put nearly a half

million sea miles under the keels of their ships. The
world is richer for that voyaging!

They made friends with the descendants of the
Bounty mutineers on Pitcairn Island— a place they visited for twenty-five years. In 1934 they rescued shipwrecked Pitcairn Islanders and a Polynesian girl. While
returning them to Pitcairn, Captain Johnson performed
the marriage ceremony to unite a descendant of the
Bounty's crew and a girl from Manga Reva. Seven of
their Christmases were spent in the barren Galapagos
Islands, where they found endless fascination in marine
life among the rocks. They danced on the beach by moon-
light in Tahiti, fished by torchlight in sailing outrigger
canoes in the Filberts, hobnobbed with "wild men" in
the New Hebrides, sat in on a royal cremation in Bali.

The voyaging was not uneventful. They hit an un-
charted reef in the open sea east of the Solomons, got
a twisted rudder post in the Indian Ocean, encountered cyclones, and carried away topmasts ("always at
night," as Captain Johnson has noted ruefully), losing
on the average almost one a voyage. The lost topmasts
were replaced in whatever odd corner of the world
ocean they were lost in. The *Yankee*s were sailed with
zest, the brigantine *Yankee* carrying studdingsails in
the Trade Winds, but safely, no life being lost, no major injury occurring in all those years of hard sailing
around the world.

The third *Yankee*, a steel ketch built in Holland to

the Johnsons' order, was built to traverse the rivers and canals of Europe. In seventeen years' sailing, she crossed the continent twenty-eight times, navigating some 7,000 locks, "almost part of barge life," as Irving and Exy wrote of the experience lately, ". . . buying pigeons, honey and vegetables from country lock keepers, watching blue-pinafored children cross the old stone bridges toward school and cows heading home over the same bridges at day's end."

But the third *Yankee*'s voyaging was not confined to this; in fact she sailed from Trondheim, Norway, to Wadi Halfa in the African Sudan. The Scandinavian skerries knew her sails, and the muddy reaches of the Nile. She ranged the Mediterranean, sailing in the wake of Phoenician traders, Venetian argosies and Barbary pirates, gathering fresh-eyed learning which Captain Johnson shared with those who sailed with him and with a wider audience through lectures, books and articles.

In 1975 the Johnsons sold this third *Yankee*, seeing her into good hands. "We wanted this change while we were still going strong," they said, "and so it has worked out." They "retired" to Hadley on the banks of the Connecticut River, where Captain Johnson's family has lived for more than a hundred years.

But somehow the spring of 1976 found them at sea in the Mediterranean, sailing aboard Dr. George Nichols's Baltic barkentine *Regina Maris*. (Captain Johnson, lending a hand stowing sail aloft, was shown how to do it right by one of the young women working alongside him on the yard.*) Before the summer of the Tall Ships ended, Captain Johnson had sailed in Russia's *Kruzenshtern*, the former German *Padua* and the last ship of *Peking*'s class still under sail. And Christmas found the Johnsons not in the Galapagos, but on a cruise to the Antarctic. Returning toward Argentina they actually landed on and hiked around Cape Horn Island!

Captain Johnson is student as well as maker of sea history. Long a Trustee of Mystic Seaport in Connecticut, he is also Trustee of the Sea Education Association, and he serves on the Advisory Committee of the South Street Seaport Museum, where his *Peking* continues her voyage through time today. Her message is one too important for the world to lose, as he knows.

He went to sea in *Peking* to get that message.

"She was queen of the seas, and knew it," he says of his old ship. "How one hates to leave a ship like that after long months of voyaging in her, sometimes with only her own staunchness between one and death. We had been well battered in the old vessel, but we had fallen in love with her, and she had been our protecting home to a degree that no home on land could ever equal."

* * * * *

*Captain Johnson loved to tell this story. The young person knew the trick of dealing with the encumbrance of the reefed-in studdingsail boom—a spar not carried in the *Peking*, and sent up only when the sail was set in the brigantine *Yankee*.

Last fall, Captain Johnson was the guest of honor at a dinner of the American Sail Training Association held at Mystic Seaport. He talked of what he had learned in his seafaring, beginning with the ever-memorable voyage in *Peking*. There was laughter and cheering, and all hands came to their feet, as one person, when he'd done.

There was rapt silence among those sailing skippers, however, when he spoke of scenes narrated in this book: the men wrestling to secure a heavy anchor on a foredeck plunging into the winter sea, being swept away, and coming back to try again; the man working next to him snapped off the royal yard, who caught a footrope as he fell and got back on and continued his work securing a sail that was too much for the ship to carry; the ship herself, battling for life off Cape Horn, with seas crashing across her decks.

"That taught me something," said Captain Johnson to his hushed audience. "It taught me to lean forward into life."

We can be grateful that Irving Johnson does the things he does, steering a bold course in life that few among us may follow, but in whose challenge, deep learning and hard-won rewards we all may share—as we share these things in this account of his strenuous and joyous sailing in the *Peking*.

PETER STANFORD, 1977

POSTSCRIPT FOR THE SECOND EDITION

Irving Johnson died in January 1991, fourteen years after we published our first edition of this book. By then, he knew that the book had become a classic of the sail training movement in the English-speaking world and beyond. As Exy Johnson notes in her new Introduction to this edition, "The *Peking* was his university," and the life lessons he learned and came to transmit to others in his own sailing with Exy seven times around the world, and in the lectures and movie he had made with the assistance of his friend Charlie Brodhead, have spread far beyond the original crew that sailed in the vessel. The *Peking*'s voyage has passed into legend.

But it is important to remember that legends were once the rough-and-tumble, frequently contradictory reality that gave them life—if for no other reason than to make the connections to our own lives right now. And we're lucky that the cheerful shipmate "Charlie" who made the voyage with Irving, still walks this earth. In this new edition we add his commentary to this yarn.

Irving's closing years were full of activity. One remembers him driving miles on a stormy night from his family farm on the Connecticut River at South Hadley, Massachusetts, to show his film of the voyage to a group assembled aboard the *Peking* in her berth at the South Street Seaport Museum in New York. Alfred Kirchhoff, one of Irving's shipmates in the *Peking*, had come down from his home in Vermont unbeknownst to Irving. He startled Irving by correcting him on some minor point in the film's narration, speaking from the back of the crowded, darkened Liverpool house—the midship crew space where the film was being shown.

Nearly half a century, and the most terrible of wars, had passed between the two men since they had last met. Their reunion was an awesome and joyous occasion—not just for the two men, but for all who were present!

The peace-loving Irving had signed up in the US Navy as Lieutenant Commander as the clouds of World War II darkened the horizon. His special mission was to develop accurate surveys of the Pacific islands, in case the Navy would have to fight over them in the spreading conflict. "Probably," notes Exy, "we had been to more islands than anyone else in the world."

Irving was at Pearl Harbor on the quiet Sunday morning of 7 December 1941—and I remember his expression of horror when he described the thick black columns of smoke rising from the port as Japanese aircraft inflicted grievous losses on the US fleet. He knew, he said, that he was looking at the funeral pyre of great ships and brave men. Assigned to a survey ship to do his vital charting work, he rose to command his own ship in the Navy and retired with the rank of Captain, USNR.

After the war he and Exy picked up the threads of their life where they had left off. They bought a new *Yankee* to replace the wooden schooner they'd sailed in the 1930s. This was a steel ship rigged as a brigantine, in which they resumed their round-the-world voyages, picking up where they had left off when the whole Pacific and Atlantic worlds were turned into ferociously contested battlegrounds.

Then there was Irving receiving our James Monroe Award, not for his leadership in sail training, but for his superbly accurate, enthusiasm-generating work in recording what he'd learned on film, on paper, and in his talks which lived on in the minds of all who heard him. He and Exy walked back up Pearl Street from India House, in Lower Manhattan, where the presentation had been made, to South Street to visit his old ship. On the way Irving and Exy took turns telling me how important was the work that we were doing in the National Maritime His-

Exy and Irving at the presentation of the
James Monroe Award to Irving in 1977

torical Society, and in publishing the Society's magazine *Sea History*. "You mustn't ever give up," said Irving. "Keeping at it wins out in the end, if you put your heart in what you're doing." I remember Exy said she wished they could do more to help in these endeavors.

But of course in giving us this book, and in contributing that magnificent Afterword you'll find at the end, they did a great deal to help our then-struggling Society and its new-fledged magazine. And the help so cheerfully given, and in such seamanlike fashion, lives on.

Among the patrons of this new edition, whose contributions made possible its publication, is Alix Thorne of New Hampshire. With her husband Dan she is a leading light of the awakening world of sail training, where more and more young people ("young people of all ages," as the American Sail Training Association likes to say) are finding sea legs for life by getting down to fundamentals, voyaging in deep water and shoal under sail. This, after all, was how the world was opened to mankind, and how we, the human race, discovered the planet's shape and features, and how mankind came to encounter itself in all our endless variety. Retracing those footsteps across the trackless sea is no bad way to come to know something very basic in the human story, and things basic in ourselves.

Alix, writing in praise of "her favorite book," told us of her sailing summer, remarking that her 16-year-old son, Will Hornblower, was off to sail in Norway's able full-rigger *Sørlandet*. The Johnson legend lives on! And Irving still challenges us to "lean forward into life" in these pages, with the same spirit and drama he showed the first time I heard him utter those words.

> PETER STANFORD, President
> National Maritime Historical Society
> Autumn 1995

NOTE: *The* Peking *may be visited today at the South Street Seaport Museum, 207 Front Street, New York, NY 10038. And Mystic Seaport Museum distributes a videotape of Irving Johnson's film "The* Peking *Battles Cape Horn," also available packaged with this book. Write Mystic Seaport Museum, Mystic, Connecticut 06355.*

INTRODUCTION

THE *PEKING* WAS HIS UNIVERSITY

In the time since Irving died (1991) I have given much thought not only to him, but to his life as a whole. Few people are able to use their full talents happily in their way of life. This was his great blessing.

Fortunately, we both believed in and wanted the same thing: to sail the two big *Yankees* around the world with their amateur crews. The whole romance of the Age of Sail affected us both. In me Irving did not need a First Mate. I am not one of those for whom "happiness is my hand on the tiller." Though the public assumes I am a great sailor, that I am not. However, I was happy in the sailing life. I always stood regular watches, four on and eight off, because anything else for me would have lost the way we were all crew. I am so glad I didn't just come on deck when the sailing was beautiful or especially exciting.

Apart from sailing talent, I could contribute to the ship in other ways. She needed everything both of us could give.

Irving used to say he didn't want to go to college because they didn't teach what he wanted to learn. How true. The *Peking* was his university. His preparation was the five years he spent skippering yachts—"after I realized people would pay you to sail." Even more were the springs and falls fitting out and laying up at Herreshoff's yard where standards were of the highest and the older men around him were expert riggers.

Our timing, too, was most fortunate. We could go anywhere and just drop the hook. Today there seem to be many places it is better not to go and there are restrictions we didn't have to consider. In the ketch *Yankee* also, the timing was right. We explored Europe's inland waterways before that wonderful experience became popular, before there were charter boats and hotel barges available. Lockkeepers were pleased to see our "joli bateau" and the American flag. We made friends as we crossed back and forth across Europe, though not always by the same route. Incidentally, I became a very good hand on the ketch.

Exy at the helm of *Wander Bird*,
with Irving at her side, in San Francisco Bay, 1986.

Once a sailing friend said, as Irving had of *Peking*'s Captain Jurs, "There was always a bit of Irving aboard our boat," a nice compliment.

I see I have used the word *fortunate* more than once. There was so much of that in Irving's life.

ELECTA (EXY) JOHNSON
South Hadley, Massachusetts
Spring 1995

Tug towing the *Peking* down the Elbe

I

THE *PEKING* LEAVES PORT ON A FRIDAY

YACHTING was my summer job, and in the colder half of the year I liked to rove around and see the world. The summer cruising was confined to the New England coast, which was all right enough, but I had a hankering to make a long voyage in one of the old-time square-riggers.

To do that was not easy. Neither the United States nor England had any square-rigged sailing-ships left, and it looked as if such an experience as I wanted, soon would be impossible. But Germany still had a few of these vessels, and they were big four-masted barks that made voyages round Cape Horn to Chile. So in the autumn of 1929, after I had attended to laying up the yacht of which I was captain, I started for Germany.

Charlie, a pal of mine, went with me. He had just graduated from Princeton, and we were about the same age. What he wanted was a period of adventure before starting to teach history. He had been on the college track team as a long distance runner, and he had been two years on the 'Varsity wrestling team. Well, I was something of a wrestler myself, and I said, "I guess we can make things interesting for each other or any one who wants to tackle us."

We wandered around for a while in the British Isles, and another while on the continent before going to Hamburg; and among the places that we visited was the Giants Causeway on the north coast of Ireland. While there my hat was blown off into the big waves caused by a storm, and was carried far out from shore. Close by where I stood watching the receding hat, was a wishing-spring and a stone wishing-seat.

Charlie waved toward them saying: "No need to shed any tears. There's your chance to get back your hat."

"Why, sure it is," I said laughing. "At any rate I'll try them."

All that I had to do was to drink from the spring and then sit in the stone seat and wish that my hat would come back. Apparently that didn't influence the hat a particle, and we gave it up; but we continued to loiter about for a half hour or so exploring the great, rock-pillared Causeway. Then—believe it or not—I saw my hat heaving close to the shore; and I caught up a stick, followed a retreating wave, and fished the hat out onto the rocks.

"Well done!" Charlie cried. "And now that you've proved that the wishing apparatus here delivers the goods, why don't you wish for something else?"

"Good idea," I said. "That's just what I'll do."

So I drank from the magic spring, then sat in the stone seat and said, "I wish for plenty of exciting storms on our voyage round Cape Horn."

About three weeks later we arrived in Hamburg one morning and looked about us. We saw a great commercial city which is one of the most important of European ports. It occupies both sides of the River Elbe and nearly surrounds the harbor. Docks abounded set at all angles, and canals reached back into the city. Motor boats were buzzing around, and tugs and lighters enlivened the harbor, along the borders of which lay big vessels from many distant ports. Among these was the largest sailing ship in the world, the *Peking,* on which we were to voyage more than eleven thousand miles to Chile.

At the offices of the company that owned the *Peking* and four other sister vessels, the official with whom we dealt expressed a great deal of surprise that we should want to make such a trip.

"It never has been done before," he said again and again, looking very grim, and he made it plain that we were being given an exceptional privilege.

We were to go as sailors, but not to be tied very closely to the routine work. Consequently, we had to pay a moderate sum for our passage.

The official still looked unhappy when we were parting from him, and he was so convinced that we didn't realize what we were getting in for that he made a serious effort to dissuade us from going.

"It will be cold and stormy," he said, "and if you are sick you won't get the care you are used to. You will have rough quarters and coarse food. And you must remember, that once started, you will have to keep on to the end. The ship can't put into port to let you off."

I turned to Charlie. "Do you want to quit?" I asked.

"Of course not," he said. "I didn't come for a boatride on a millpond."

"We're going anyway," I told the official.

Then he started another tune, saying: "But do you understand the danger? Last year one of our ships—big, just like the *Peking*—sunk going round Cape Horn. She lost her masts overboard in a storm, and as the masts went they ripped up the deck so she began to go down. But there was time to rig the radio on the stump of one of the masts, and help came. The same season a big Danish ship left Buenos Aires headed for Australia by way of the Horn. Nothing has been heard of her since." He looked at us questioningly.

"I don't know but you are right," I said. "Still we've kind of made up our minds to take the chances, whatever they may be. Isn't that so Charlie?" I asked, turning to him.

"Yes, that's about the way of it," he agreed.

The expression of disapproval continued to linger on the official's face, but he shook hands and we parted.

Charlie seemed to be in a very serious mood that evening when we got back to the little hotel where we were staying for the few days before the ship sailed. Presently he wrote something with great care on a sheet of paper and passed it over to me. "My will," he said.

"Isn't this kind of sudden?" I asked. "What's up?"

"It's the things that man said to us at the shipping office," he replied. "They've got on my nerves. I'm not wanting to back out, but I do want to send my will home."

He asked me to sign it as a witness, and I accommodated him. Then he went out and mailed it in a street post office box and came back more cheerful.

The *Peking* was moored a little way out in the harbor, and we went to her in a motor boat. She was "a great big wagon!!" Her hull, masts, and yards were steel, and I never had seen rigging better cared for. She was built in 1911 and had been kept in fine condition.

We bought working clothes and extra blankets, and a moving picture camera. But what we most appreciated of the things we took on board was a Christmas box sent to Hamburg from home. It was our guess that there were good things to eat inside.

We met the captain in his cabin the first time we were on the vessel. He was like his ship—big!—had big hands and a big smile, in fact was big in every way. He said he used to be mate of the *Prussian,* a five mast full rigged ship. It was while he was first officer on her about 1912 that she was lost in a storm on the English coast.

He knew English pretty well because he had been in England some and had made voyages with American sailors; but in recent years he had used it so little he was out of practice. Spanish was the foreign language he knew best, and he kept mixing Spanish words into his talk. The Spanish had been picked up at the time of the World War. The war caught his ship on the open sea, and he took refuge in the Canary Islands where he stayed four years waiting for it to end.

The day of our first call on the captain we went back to shore in the boat of a company

---

*In a rare error, Captain Johnson has this wrong. The *Preussen* was rammed by a steamer in 1910. With bowsprit carried away, she could not be brought under control before drifting ashore in the English Channel near Dover. Attempts to pull her off proved unavailing.

official. A sailor's sea bag lay in the bottom, and I asked, "What's that bag?"

The official replied: "A lot of trouble—that's what it is. The sailor it belonged to dropped off the *Peking's* rigging into the sea on her last voyage. We have to get the bag through the customs before it can be sent to his parents."

And Charlie said in a low voice for only me to hear, "I'm glad I made my will."

Our final day in Hamburg was the last Thursday in the month. We forgot all about its being Thanksgiving Day, and we ate our dinner in one of a line of cheap fish restaurants. Each of us drank a glass of milk, and we had all we wanted of fish and chips. The chips would have been called French fried potatoes back home. They tasted fine, and so did the fish and milk, but it wasn't much of a menu for a Thanksgiving dinner.

In the evening we paid our hotel bill, picked up the few belongings that were in our room and went out to go to the ship.

"How much money have you?" I asked Charlie.

"Mighty little," he said. "I'm down almost to my last cent."

"And I'm down almost to my last pfennig," I told him.

"You're worse off than I am then," he said; because a cent is a cent, but a pfennig is only a quarter of a cent. Let's spend what's left and have one less thing to think of."

So we went into a little joint down near the waterfront, and I said to Charlie, "We'll spend all our money right here except just enough to take us out to the ship by motor boat."

After careful deliberation we bought apples and chocolate bars. Then we made our way toward the *Peking's* landing wharf, which was so moored that it rose and fell with the tide. One dim electric light was burning on the wharf, and as we approached it Charlie suddenly exclaimed, "By Jiminy! here's some more money!"

I wasn't surprised. He had a habit of slipping such coins as came to him into whatever pocket at the moment was most convenient. Now he showed me several that he had pulled out of a pocket he had missed in his earlier search. "All German," he said. "We ought to spend 'em right here in Hamburg."

"Yes," I agreed, "that's what we ought to do."

And we returned to the waterside joint, bought more apples and some cookies, and were back at the wharf in time to get the last boat to the ship.

We had expected to share the crew's quarters, but those were full, and we were assigned to a room amidships that opened off the captain's dining saloon, where we were to eat. There were two bunks, one above the other, and a settee with room underneath for such things as suitcases and sea bags. Also there were two lockers, and there was a wash basin above which a little metal lamp was fastened to the wall. The room was not heated, but probably that was better for us. We weren't so likely to catch cold when going out on deck.

Charlie looked at the bunks and asked, "How are we going to decide which will have which?"

"Let's toss a penny!" I said, and that was what we did. He won and chose the upper bunk.

We turned in early, and the next thing we knew some one stumbled into our room and gave each of us a vigorous punch. It was the mate. "I just wanted to see if you were here," he said. "The police boat is along side waiting for me to make sure that you are leaving with the vessel. We're just starting."

It was about six o'clock in the morning, and still dark. Hurrying footsteps sounded on the deck, and we were eager to see what was going on. So as soon as we could get into our working clothes up we went.

A tug had us in tow, and the vessel was sliding smoothly along down the Elbe. Back of the main mast was a double steering wheel, and as we continued down the narrow channel four men were kept busy steering. At sea it was only in storms that the *Peking* had more than one man at the wheel.

The *Peking*

Chart room on the midships deck and a sail being repaired.

Some of the 350 lines for which we had to learn the German names

A couple of the mates at different times tried to put Charlie and me to work. This would have been fine if only we could have understood their orders, which were given in German. Often we saw what to do by watching others.

Once another fellow and I bent on the outer jib. To do that we had to get up near the shark's tail at the end of the jib boom which projected beyond the bowsprit. Every old sailor thinks that a shark's tail as a jib boom decoration on a sailing ship is a necessity.

It brings fair winds, and if a new ship is sailing, the crew cut off the tail of the first shark they catch and nail it up in the accustomed place. Moreover, in doing this they always are careful to have the longest part of the tail point upward, for that makes fair winds more certain.

Our starting day was the last Friday in November, 1929. It was cold, and rain fell most of the time, but no one wore gloves. We could keep our hands warm enough without them when we had plenty of exercise.

Several times we saw groups of people along

the Elbe who had come to wave farewell to some
of the sailors on board. The banks were low and
the landscape monotonous. As we went on, the
stream kept broadening out until it was an inlet
from the sea and no banks at all were in sight.

The crews of the ships we met looked the *Peking* over with great interest, and well they might,
she was so big and her masts were such sky-
scrapers! The only sail we set was the inner
jib, but all the yards were hauled around to catch
the wind and help the tug along. The crew didn't
know what to make of me—pulling on a line
with them one minute, and the next minute taking moving pictures of them.

In the middle of the afternoon, sixty-five miles
from Hamburg, we anchored at Cuxhaven near
the mouth of the river to add a lot of airplane
gasoline to our cargo. It was in fifty gallon
drums, and a lighter brought it out to us.

Near each hatch was a one cylinder Diesel
engine for use in loading and unloading cargo
in South America. One of these was put into
action to get the drums of gasoline down into the

hold. As soon as we put to sea the engines had to be partly dismantled to save them from damage by the waves. So the good old capstan bars were in constant use from the time we left port.

The *Peking* was loaded to capacity, or "down to her marks," as the seamen say. The marks were two parallel white lines about a foot long and six inches apart painted on the hull amidships. They showed the depth to which the law allowed the vessel to be loaded. The hull was painted black, and the masts were painted a buff tint. Buff is used so commonly on ships for the purpose, that it is the custom of the sea to speak of it as "mast color."

We had a general cargo of everything from a couple of hundred tons of coke to one hundred and fifty porcelain toilets. Our full load made the ship more comfortable to live in because her motions were slower, but it was bound to let tremendous seas wash over the deck if we had rough weather. The main deck at the lowest point, was only five feet above water level. However, she looked higher-sided because there were five feet of bulwarks. She was drawing twenty-four feet of water, and that was too much for her to make her best speed.

When we were once more under way I started on a journey up the main mast to the royal yard, which is above all others near the top of the mast. About a third of the distance up I came to the futtock shrouds and found there wasn't any lubber hole in the top to climb through. This meant that the only way to go up was to cling to the futtock shrouds which slanted backward like the under side of a ladder. I kept on until I was on the royal yard. If I had gone up in a building, I would have been seventeen stories high. To get up to such a height on a ship, where there were no elevators, was an awful climb. I was tired and all out of breath. But after a short rest I lay out along the yard—that is, leaned over on it and slid my feet along the footropes. I did that for practice and to look around.

It gave me a queer feeling there in mid air, with a network of rigging round about, and the ship down below gliding through the water. She

She looked strangely distant and so narrow

The whole crew

Bending a new fores'l. It weighed a ton.

looked strangely distant and so narrow as to be incapable of supporting such a quantity of masts, yards, and rigging.

After a while I noticed far below me twenty or more sailors who were strung along a yard bending the mains'l. I climbed down, took the position next to the end, and did my best without any instruction. Night was coming on when the task was started, and after working two hours we had to go by feel! The darker it got the more yelling there was among us, and from officers on the deck below.

One of the sailors told me to cut a certain line while we were up there. I was proud of having a good, sharp knife handy, and I "whips it out" and cut the line. The sailor must have made some mistake, for no sooner was the cutting done than down fell half the sail.

There was considerable talk about that little operation, because the sail had to be hauled back into place and it weighed nearly a ton. The fellow who ordered the cutting was blamed by the others, and perhaps I was too, but the gabble was all in German which I couldn't understand.

Before we reached the open sea we dropped anchor again. That was because of the old superstition the captain had about beginning his ocean voyage on Friday. He didn't write anything in his log book until Saturday.

After we were in our bunks that night I said to Charlie, "It seems to me from the looks of things now that this trip is going to be wonderful."

"I'm not so sure as to what's coming to us," he responded, "but by cheese and crackers! we've had a whale of a time so far."

That cheese and crackers expression was about as near as he ever came to swearing.

Hove to in the North Sea

II

TRAPPED IN THE NORTH SEA

At daylight the next morning the tug heaved aboard her towing cable, and we hauled up our anchor. After that it didn't take us long to get out into the North Sea. In order to go faster we set all our heads'ls and stays'ls and the upper and lower spankers.

The greater part of our crew consisted of

young fellows fitting themselves to become officers, and they had to pay to go on the *Peking*
for this purpose. A number of big steamship
companies were interested in having them get
this training on a sailing ship before entering
their employ. Any old shellback will tell you
that the man who has served his time in sail is
worth two of those who have been to sea only in
steamers. We had fifty-four of these cadets whose
ages varied from fifteen to twenty-four years.
They were a pretty good type—much above the
average of sailors—intelligent and fairly well
educated. Some of them had made several trips
to Chile, but for others this was their first voyage. Besides the cadets there were five regular
sailors, the captain and four mates, two cooks, a
steward, sailmaker, carpenter, blacksmith, bo'-
son, radio operator, and Charlie and me, making a total of seventy-four.

Radio was a part of our equipment, but it
would hardly send messages more than a hundred miles even under good conditions. Except

in emergencies we would receive nothing but weather reports and time ticks.

The *Peking* certainly was a big thing to be pushed around by the wind, but she had masts and yards that were proportionately as tremendous as she was. Our three royals, the highest sails on the ship, were over one hundred and seventy-five feet above the water, and each of the three lower yards was one hundred feet long. Three hundred and forty-five feet was the ship's length over all, her width was forty-seven feet, and her cargo load four thousand, seven hundred tons.

Among the voyagers on board were about a dozen hens, three pigs, and a turkey gobbler. The pigs had a built-in steel pen just aft of the foc'sle head. The hens and turkey had their quarters near the stern in a low, strongly-built, board structure that was on top of the poop deck over the radio shack.

On the raised midships deck, back of the steering wheels, was the chart room. In it was our chronometer, and in one corner the chart table, so called, but more like a desk. The chart table had drawers in which most of the charts were kept. Other charts were rolled up and stuck in slats that covered half the ceiling. A stout swivel chair was fastened to the deck in front of the table for the skipper. There he sat while working out the sights each morning and noon, and, under exceptional conditions, in the afternoon or even at night.

In the opposite corner was a built-in settee with a leather-covered, hair-stuffed mat on it. This and a small accompanying table were used by the mates while working out their sights, which the captain always looked at as a check on his own sights and figuring.

When the weather was stormy enough so that the captain did not wish to leave the midships deck he might go into the chart room and lie down on the sofa. He could be summoned from there very quickly. The room had a signal flag locker, and the ship's clock was there, hung so that the man at the wheel could see it by looking back through a window.

We had only two sextants, and they were kept in drawers of the chart table. One was the captain's. The other belonged to the ship, and was so worn that the figures could only be read by daylight. Star sights couldn't be taken with it at all on that account.

During our first day on the North Sea I found time to go to the top of each of the four masts. Some of the ratlines were broken. They are used like the rungs of a ladder to put your feet on while climbing up and down, but a sailor never trusts them. He holds on to the shrouds at the side.

You need to look alive when clambering about up there in the rigging. It is important that one hand always should grip something, and the grip should unconsciously be tight enough to support your entire weight. "One hand for yourself and one for the ship" is the old sailors rule, but when in doubt I used two hands for myself.

We bent the last square sail that afternoon. It was one of our largest patches of canvas. Sailors call it the cro'jack, but dictionaries spell it cross-jack. The decks were given a good scrubbing, harbor gear was put away, and sailing gear was gotten out. This was the ship's first washdown after over a month in dirty ports, and she looked much better afterward.

Charlie and I spent Saturday evening in the dining saloon writing, and studying German. A fire was burning in a little stove there. It didn't give out much heat, but was better than nothing, for we were far in the north, winter had come, and the cold was of that damp, penetrating sort you never get on land. Above the big table was a large kerosene lamp hung in gimbals. Its light seemed pretty feeble to us after being accustomed to electric lighting. On the walls were two framed photographs. One portrayed the launching of the *Peking,* the other the captain's wife.

Each mate had tacked up in his room a dozen or more pictures cut out of mazagines and newspapers. Ships were the favorite subjects, particularly those in storms. The crew had very crowded quarters, and not much space was available for pictures, but they had a few that were much like those of the mates, and some others of a feminine sort for which sailors in their lonely life have perhaps more than the ordinary weakness.

We had the dining saloon to ourselves all the evening except for the captain's passing through occasionally. It was his habit to go early to bed. Sometimes he said a few words. One of his parting shots was: "Ach! Writing! And when you get back home you vill write a book with a lot of lies in it!"

Sunday morning we set all sails except the royals and cro'jack. To do this, six great steel yards had to be hoisted twenty feet up the masts so the sails could be set under them. The hoisting of each yard was done by about eight men heaving on the iron cranks of a halyard winch for nearly half an hour. The other sails dropped down from yards which were stationary, and they were easier to set.

The wind was so light it didn't drive us along enough to catch up with the tug, which is something that often happens. At noon off the Hook of Holland the tug was let go, and she circled around astern to get our letters. The captain threw a line to her and tied to it the bundle of letters so they could be hauled over to her without touching the water.

But the fellows on the tug couldn't untie his knot, and the captain wouldn't let go of his line. He told the tug crew what kind of sailors they were, and after they had listened to a few of his peppy remarks one of them got a knife from down below and cut the bundle off from the line.

Then the tug blew three blasts on her whistle, to which we responded with three blasts of our fog horn; and we gave three cheers which brought answering cheers from the tug crew. When these ceremonies had been attended to the tug steamed away to Lands End, England, where she would wait for a ship to tow back.

She could have taken us along, but if we had a favorable wind a two-days' voyage would put us well past Dover where we would have no further need of a tug, and the owners of the *Peking* wanted to economize.

Several times the wind changed, and then died down. Oh, what a job it was to shift all the yards and sails from one tack to the other! Each time it kept thirty men busy about an hour before everything was done. This needn't have taken more than fifteen minutes if all hands had been used to it. We lay becalmed for several hours, and then picked up a north-northwest slant that sent us briskly along toward the English Channel.

The sailmaker and I became friends that day. He had been on an American ship and could speak passable English. Just after dinner I happened along where he was seated on his bench patching a sail, and I stopped to watch the process.

He looked up and said, "Mahl-zeit!"

"What does that mean?" I asked.

And he replied, "Dot means all der same like, 'I hope your food will set well on your stomach.' In my country we often say dot to somebody just going to eat or just through eating."

We still were talking when I chanced to sneeze.

Instantly the sailmaker exclaimed, "Gesundheit!" And he added "Dot is vot ve speak if a friend he sneeze. It means 'I vish you are not going to have a bad cold,' or, as many people vill tell you, 'Heaven forbid that the devil should get into you!'"

In the days that followed he fell into the habit of wishing me good luck whenever he saw me either going to eat or coming from eating, or when he heard me sneeze. This always put me in a good humor and must have helped my digestion if there were any need of such help, which I doubt.

The sailmaker was stocky, yet quick-motioned, and he was jolly, sociable, and accommodating. Usually he had a smile on his face. At the time of the World War he worked in a Zeppelin factory, but most of his forty or fifty years had been spent at sea where his experiences included all kinds of long voyages, storms, and shipwrecks. He told about a sailor's falling

Furling the royal 175 feet from the deck

Repairing cargo slings on and near the forehatch

The sailmaker and his helpers

overboard on the last voyage of the *Peking*. A lifeboat was launched, but couldn't find a trace of the poor fellow.

The sailmaker showed me a notebook in which he had written about his various voyages. In 1911 the ship he was on started Friday and was wrecked a few days later. Another Friday start on a voyage was made in 1924. It caused a broken rudder. After that had been fixed, the ship hadn't gone far when along came a worse storm and wrecked her. In each case about half the crew was lost. Both dates were underscored in red, and so was the Friday when the *Peking* left port on our trip.

He didn't think that the vessel's stop over night at the mouth of the Elbe would change the day of our start, as recorded in the log of whatever power it is that links a voyage begun on Friday with the vessel's shipwreck.

"It was on a Friday," he said, "dot we left our port, Hamburg, and whether dot was in der captain's log or not will make no difference. Re-

member vot I say. I haf had experiences. We
will be shipwrecked."

Early the next morning life lines were rigged
along both sides of the forward and after decks.
They were just above one's head, and were very
useful for clinging to in bad weather. Another
precaution was the stringing of nets about two
feet high at the top of the bulwarks to catch any
of us who were swept off our feet by big waves
washing across the decks.

The wind gradually got stronger until at
eleven in the morning it was coming with a rush.
Then there were great doings! The order was
given to take in the to'gans'ls.

We were diving into quite a sea and taking
water over forward and aft. I went aloft to help
with the sails. It gives one a sort of light feeling to be a hundred and forty feet from the water
on a perch which is jumping this way and that,
and every other way.

Meanwhile you are standing on a wire and
pulling on a flapping sail with both hands so
that every time you pull, up goes the footrope

and you nearly take a header over the yard. Such a header has been taken many a time, but never told about by the one who took it.

By the time we had finished furling the upper to'gans'l, the lower one was clewed up—that is, it was hauled up close to the yard with clewlines and buntlines leading to the deck. I shifted down to the lower yard to help furl the sail on top of it.   As I slid out on the foot rope, bending over between the to'gans'l yards, some inexperienced hand on deck let go the weather upper to'gans'l brace, and the huge steel yard came crunching down on my back with every roll of the ship.

It crushed me until I thought I would pop with the pressure, but the ends of the yards hit just in time to save me from being killed. The rest of the fellows set up a great holler until the yard was steadied. More sailors came out on the yard then and we finished furling the sail.

There is a tremendous amount of hauling and pulling done on lines and sails in such operations as these. We kept furling sails until the only ones left set were the tops'ls, three stays'ls, the fores'l, and one jib and a spanker. The breeze got so strong that when facing it we had to suck in air through our teeth, and only saved our hats by stuffing them in our pockets.

The spanker topmast stays'l was poorly furled; so the captain made us furl it again, while he gave orders in his best deep sea style. Even then he wasn't suited, and he got up on the stay and furled the sail alone. This was a pretty difficult thing to do on account of the position he had to work in, but he did a fine job.

Late in the afternoon we took in all the stays'ls and the spanker to wear ship. There seemed to be forty things going on at the same time, and in the confusion I helped as well as I could by simply doing what I saw others doing.

When hauling around the big fores'l it got to slatting because some one at the foc'sle capstan let the tack go too soon. About ten men gripped the capstan bars and began pushing around to take in on the sheet. That would save the sail if they worked fast enough. A capstan naturally is

Heaving down the foretack on the foc'sle head

Overhauling the forward capstan

The foremast with yards set corkscrew fashion

slow, but with the captain yelling his head off, and the mate cracking on the back or head each man heaving at the bars, they whirled in a way that would have made a merry-go-round dizzy.

Charlie was one of them. He said it was like the last quarter of a five-mile footrace. Every time as they raced round and came to the wire they were hauling on, they went over it flying, clearing a ten-foot space of deck at one hop.

I helped steer for a while, but wasn't lashed as were the two other men at the wheel. The lashing was to keep them from being jerked over the wheel when a big sea kicked the rudder. Steering is no soft job. The strain on one's arms makes them ache most of the time.

Extra lashings were put on all the lifeboats, spare lines were carried below, and the poultry house was covered. The mate said we were having regular North Sea weather—by which was meant a southwest gale with rain-squalls, and short, steep, high seas.

We saw forty or fifty fishing-boats hove to. They did a regular hop, skip, and jump over the waves and kept their decks fairly dry. They were ketch-rigged, and all of them were riding out the gale with their mizzen set.

This was our first really rough weather, and several of the new boys turned green around the gills and had to lean over the lee rail. Many of the older fellows laughed at them, but the sea-sick cadets didn't pay any attention. They wouldn't have cared if the ship had sunk.

In the night the wind blew itself out, and Tuesday opened with a smooth sea and a light southerly wind. The three pigs were allowed to run about the fore deck, and the poultry were let out aft. Our feathered creatures had to be kept inside when the wind blew hard lest they should be blown off the deck.

One very lively member of the ship's family was Mauritz, the captain's short-haired, tan and white, mongrel dog. He did his best to bite the pigs, but he couldn't get a good hold. They ran to get away from him and made such a racket with their squealing that they roused everybody on board.

The favorable weather gave the sailors a chance to put a lot of chafing gear on the fore-stays and forward shrouds of each mast. It had all been taken off in port to keep it clean.

I often had read of sailors coming down a backstay, and I thought I would like to try it myself. But when I came down from a height of one hundred and seventy-five feet in the good old fashioned way, hand over hand, the captain was rather huffy with me.

"I don't vant dot dose cadets should be doing such risky stunts," he said. "You vas setting dose poys a bad example."

Every morning, so far, our breakfast fare had been steak and plenty of bread, butter, cold meats, and cheese. At noon there was soup, and the soup-bone was served besides, so that we could whack off with a knife whatever hunks of meat still clung to it. Other items in the noon bill of fare were meat with gravy, potatoes, a vegetable, and lastly, a dessert of cookies, pie, or cake. There was neither bread nor butter, but

we got them for supper, together with hash, or
stew, or cold meat and potatoes.

The crew had the same variety in food that we
had, but the amount they were served was limited, while we in the captain's dining saloon were
free to take all we wanted. Down in the storeroom were three hundred and twenty bushels of
potatoes, and enough other provisions for nine
months. If all the crew ate as much as I did, I
thought the food wouldn't last more than half
that long.

Every day I would go to the chart room to
look at the charts and see where we were and
what harbors and shoals were in our vicinity.
Once I said to the captain that I wished I had
brought along my sextant that I had used on
other ships. "I'd like the practice of taking
sights," I told him.

He at once gave me permission to use the
ship's sextant, and after that I took sights rather
frequently.

When the *Peking* left port she had a mechan-
ical taffrail log at the stern to measure the ship's

The first mate teasing Mauritz

The captain, also called the skipper,
or "the old man"

The *Peking*

speed through the water. But the waves in one of the storms broke this log, and after that we had to use the old-time chip log. The apparatus was interesting, and so was the "heaving of the log" which had to be done every four hours.

Each time two sailors brought up from below a large reel with the log line on it. The line was a woven cord, about the thickness of a lead pencil and 420 feet long. At intervals of practically twenty-eight feet was a knot in the line, and at the line's free end was tied the chip. This was a thin, triangular piece of wood six inches or so across, and its lower edge was weighted with lead to keep it upright in the water, while three cords that attached it to the main line made the chip drag at right angles to the course of the ship.

The mate who had charge of operations saw to it that one of the crew was close at hand with a small sandglass, and that the two men with the reel in their hands stood ready to watch the line and see that it ran smoothly. Reckoning began only after the chip log was thrown overboard and the line had been allowed to run out past the wake of the ship to the first knot. The mate had been watching intently and with the arrival of that knot he called out, "Turn!"

Instantly the sailor who was holding the glass turned it, and waited the fourteen seconds that the sand was running down. Then he hollered, "Stop!" and the mate grabbed the line that had been running out and gave it a quick jerk. That released a peg in the log, and allowed the chip to lie flat so the apparatus could easily be drawn through the water back to the ship by the men at the reel.

Then the mate noted the number of knots in the line that had passed over the taffrail during that fourteen seconds. Those showed the speed of the vessel in nautical miles per hour. If the mate thought there had been changes in speed since the last reckoning, he had to guess how much that should modify the record of the present heaving of the log.

The currents in the North Sea are very irre-gular, and a change of wind often shifts them from their normal direction. As a result we seldom knew just where we were. One evening the captain and the mates thought we were thirty or forty miles from our actual position. They mistook North Hinder lightship for another.

I convinced them that they were wrong, and they wore ship in a hurry. Afterward they wanted to head for the lightship, but it was out of sight by then, and none of them had taken a bearing of it. I had taken one for my own satisfaction; so they used that.

Charlie and I weren't obliged to stand on watch, but we did sometimes for the fun of it, or to be with the cadets at night learning German while standing watch with them. We would have gotten along faster in this language business if it hadn't been for the captain.

He wanted to brush up his English, and he talked it to us, and told us to talk it to him. In a month or so the brushing up had made him fairly expert. Two of the mates spoke English pretty well, and all of the cadets had studied it from three to six years, but only four or five could speak it.

I started my German education by learning the names for our thirty-two sails. That was some job, but easy compared with learning the names later of the more than three hundred and fifty lines used in handling the sails.

Those lines all had to be known by the feel, so that in a squall during a pitch black night we wouldn't let go the wrong one. When our hands were too cold for feeling, we used our wrists to tell the difference between manila and hemp lines. A slight variation in the size of these lines also was a help.

Furling the fore-royal

III

FRIDAY THE THIRTEENTH

WE got down past Dover some hours before daylight on the morning of December 4th, and only three miles more would put us past the end of a shoal into a broader part of the English Channel. But the wind changed, and we were obliged to go back into the North Sea.

The number of shoal places in the Channel

near Dover and in the neighboring part of the North Sea is surprising, and a dozen or more lightships are stationed there to warn the many vessels that pass to and fro on those waters.

We shortened down to lower tops'ls and the fores'l while running north out of the Channel. The only thing we could do was to tack around in the North Sea until the wind became favorable again. This has been known to take weeks —and the weather report for the next day was southwest gales.

Our fresh meat was all gone, and that pleased the captain because he liked the good old salt horse better. We had pickled herring for supper and it went very well, but I wouldn't want it fed to me at home, or salt horse either. We were told that our salt horse was partly salt beef, but it was tough enough to be all horse and old horse at that.

Sure enough, the gales came the next day, and they were from the southwest, which was the course we wanted to steer. There was great excitement about noon when we took in the fores'l. The shouting and yelling of the captain and mates could be heard even above the slatting of the great sail that was causing all the excitement.

Everyone pulled like mad at the buntlines and clewlines. When those were made fast, we climbed up on the yard and found the heavy canvas extra stiff from the soaking it was getting with salt spray. After a long time it was furled on the yard, and we hove to under lower tops'ls, inner jib, and spanker stays'l.

Seas came over the rail once in a while, but the ship rode the waves better than any vessel I had seen before. A number eight to nine gale probably was what we were having. It whistled a wild yet merry tune in the rigging, but the noise didn't reach us when we were below deck. Down there we wouldn't have known that the wind was anything more than an ordinary breeze.

I put in an hour or so at sail-making every day, and always did it after dark so I wouldn't miss any interesting daylight sights or happenings.

Friday was a fine clear day, but with a strong southwest wind that didn't do us any good. I went around with a group of first trip boys learning the names and positions of various lines. When the captain yelled at them they were scared into such confusion they didn't know their heads from their feet.

We had been driven a long way north, and that night there was another gale. How the wind did whistle! Once in a while a sea caught somebody in the neck and sent him flying.

Our red and green sidelights were in danger. They were hung in their usual place on the foc'sle head, but the waves now coming over the bow were so big and threatening that we hoisted the lights from below into the light towers at the sides of the foc'sle head. There they were protected by metal and thick glass.

We had a regular he-man's gale Saturday. I went up the foremast to help make fast the upper tops'l which had worked loose. While climbing up, if the ship rolled to windward, I had to push down to keep from being blown up the mast.

A sixty-foot ketch-rigged fishing boat crossed close to our stern and was making nice weather of it, considering the size of the boat. We were being driven to leeward, while she, with power to help, was gaining a little.

Two of our men were steering lashed at the wheel. Each had a stout canvas strap over his shoulder that went down to an eyebolt in the deck. If it hadn't been for the lashing, the wheel would have chucked them overboard when it kicked.

One of the men didn't steer well, and the captain took a poke at his jaw to encourage him to do better. But the poke missed the mark, and the captain's other big fist bent the fellow up by hitting him in the stomach.

The captain was a whole show when he was mad—yelling, cursing, stamping the deck, and waving his arms. If ever there was a real, husky old sea-dog, he was one, standing six feet and two inches, weight two hundred and forty pounds, hands the largest I ever have seen, and his thumb nearly two inches wide. Except for a small mustache and goatee, he was clean shaven.

Charlie was sitting at the end of the table when I came below for dinner, and just then a huge sea heaved the ship over so he had to spread out his arms to catch the dishes. "Hold her, Charlie, she's a ra'rin'!" I called out. He had enough to do without making any reply.

The wave swept up on the midships deck, and a couple of buckets of cold North Sea water spurted down through cracks in the skylight onto Charlie as he heroically clung to the dishes. Fortunately he had the aid of some stout racks that had been fastened on the table to keep things from sliding off.

Late in the day eight of us were up on the foc'sle head hauling in the inner jib sheet. But we found this couldn't be done by hand, and we were making ready to do the hauling with the capstan when a sea swept over us. Every man held on as tightly as he could, but tenpins never upended any quicker. We were all torn loose

On the end of the royal yard

A heavy sea rolling aboard

and swept along in a twirling smother until I
thought I must be overboard.

Then bang! my head hit something hard, and
my whole body was jammed beneath—I didn't
know-what. When the water drained off I found
myself under a small tank. All my bones seemed
to be intact, and I got onto my feet.

The captain and several others were aft looking over the side of the ship to see if any one
were overboard. They only saw a hat that had
been washed off from some fellow's head.

My companions were tangled up in the high
iron railing, which had strained them out from
the smothering water as a net does fish. One of
them was the second mate. He hadn't moved
when I got to him. I shook him, and he opened
his eyes. "Have you broken your leg?" I asked.

He just groaned. His leg was twisted through
the iron railing, and that was what saved him
from going overboard. Luckily it hadn't broken,
and his worst injury was a wrenched hip. Two
fellows had their faces mashed enough to be

sent aft to the captain, and I got a bad black eye, and a crack on the jaw that opened the skin some.

But I stayed with the others heaving on the capstan bars until the sheet broke. Then we had to lower the sail and furl it.

I expected we would let well enough alone, stay off from the foc'sle head and leave the sail down. But no, the second mate, in spite of the way the sea had misused him, limped along leading the way down to the storeroom where we got out a new sheet. This we rove off in place of the broken one, then set the sail, and hauled in on the sheet with the capstan.

The new sheet held. We had been on the foc'sle head at our task for a half hour, but no wave the size of that other happened to come over.

As I went aft, I vowed that in future when I was where seas might come over, I would try to have a place picked out to wind myself up on in a hurry. I had a good suit of oilskins, but it would take a diving suit to keep out water such as we had been in lately.

Sunday came with moderate southwest gales and some heavy squalls. In one of these squalls the mizzen topmast stays'l halyard parted, and before it could be taken in the sail was blown to shreds.

The large seas got quite playful at times. There was one that lifted a three-ton anchor which was catted over the bow. When the anchor came down it broke the heavy chain lashing, but the fall had been checked so that two manila hawsers, which were on as preventer lashings, held it. Otherwise it probably would have punched a hole in our bow.

At once the mate and several sailors hurried to put on more rope and wire lashings, and there was no hesitation, though they knew that death would come to all of them, if, while at their task there came another wave such as had jumped the six thousand pound anchor. Men have no chance when a solid sea strikes them, but they worked as only sailing-ship men can for the safety of their vessel.

We had two of those anchors, and carried

eighteen hundred feet of chain for them. The metal of the links was three inches in diameter.

During the North Sea gales that had assailed us so persistently, Charlie and I had been learning a lot of German swear words. We couldn't help it, they were used so freely to describe the weather and to indicate how cold the swearers felt.

One morning, just after breakfast when Charlie was wearing his last dry clothes, he stepped out on deck without putting on any oil-skins. An old grayback came over the rail and soaked him from head to foot. I couldn't help laughing at the expression on his face when he stumbled into the cabin after his wetting.

"What's the matter, Charlie?" I said. "Are you one of those fellows who believe in having an ice-water shower before breakfast?"

"Oh, can that! You'll get yours next," he retorted.

The captain opened the slop chest as was the custom on Sunday. "Slops" are all kinds of working-clothes, knives, pipes, tobacco, and other small stores, and the crew bought eagerly. When the captain got tired of handing out the merchandise he closed the chest and said there would be no more sold until next week.

Those who hadn't had a chance to buy were out of luck, and one of them started to protest, but the captain yelled "Raus!" That meant "Get out!" and it caused more action than any other one word I ever had heard.

The sailmaker said that starting Friday on this voyage was the cause of all the gales that had assailed us. "This ship never will get back to Hamburg," he declared with great seriousness.

The captain, too, was now saying that we should not have started on so unlucky a day—it made certain our having bad weather. There was no joking when they talked about it either.

The funny thing was the captain's evident conclusion that his little trick with the days at the mouth of the Elbe hadn't fooled old Neptune. He was taking it for granted that our voyage had started on Friday in spite of the record

in his log. How else could such persistently out-
ragious weather be accounted for?

So much water came on deck Sunday night
that one of the pigs was drowned, and in the
morning some of the crew heaved the carcass
overboard. We put a larger chain on the anchor,
and it was properly catted again.

There was a first-rate gale with rain in the
afternoon, and I made a trip up to the mizzen
royal yard to see if I could hold on at the top of
the mast with the ship jumping around. I found
that I could, but it was tiresome going up the
mast or coming down when you had the extra
strain of pulling your legs back against the wind
for each step. In high winds we always went up
and down on the windward side of the shrouds
so as to be blown toward them and not blown off.
The rain was being driven by the wind with such
force that it felt more like hail than water.

On the way down I went out to the end of the
lower tops'l yard which carried the only sail set
on the mizzen mast. Whenever the sail shook,

the whole yard jumped and bent in so startling a manner that I hiked back to the mast in a hurry.

Just after dark there was a great bang forward. The foretopmast headstay had parted! To have such a thing as that happen in a storm made it not unlikely that we would lose all our masts. The inner jib that was set on the stay blew to smithereens, and in less than a minute there weren't five yards left of what had been over one hundred square yards of sail.

Fifteen or so of the most experienced men on board were called, to put on preventer tackles so as to make sure that the mast wouldn't go. It was a ticklish job. Rain was falling and the night was pitch black. We couldn't see ten feet. Often we couldn't see each other, and were only able to recognize another man by getting close and peering under his sou'wester.

About half the gang were on the foc'sle head, and I was with the rest out on the jib boom. We did a lot of hollering and yelling, but there was so much growling water around that we could hardly hear anything that was said.

Under the jib boom was a net in which we stood. It was there on purpose to keep sailors working in that exposed position from being washed away. The seas were constantly crashing up from below, and some of the crests splashed to my waist. So much heavy spray was blown over us that even oilskins couldn't keep the water out. Once, some one who had come near and was working elbow to elbow with me, looked up into my face.

It was the sailmaker, and he exclaimed: "Oh, oh! you should not be here. It is much bad! Vell, be sure you hang on tight!"

And away he went among the other stumbling, shadowy, oilskin-clad figures working on the jib boom. I did what I could to help, depending mostly on feeling, and on what I occasionally saw that some one else was doing. Once the ship made a dive that carried under water every man on the jib boom, and the whole lot of us came near being washed off at one swipe.

We were there for an hour getting two big tackles rigged, and the fury of the waves and wind kept my heart in my mouth most of the time, but it was great sport just the same out on that long jib boom, being given a wild ride by the plunging ship. Once my imagination went so far afield that for a moment I thought, "What if my mother could see me now?"

When we took our noon sights the next day we found that after having drifted and sailed around on the North Sea for ten days, we were ten miles back of where the tug left us. Low in the southern sky was the sun, barely twelve degrees above the horizon we were so far north. It shone only about seven hours a day.

The North Sea weather at that time of year was bitterly cold, and the wind seemed to go right through us no matter how much clothing we had on. The only times we were warm were when we wrestled with the sails or had gone to bed.

I soon learned that after parting from the tug, the ship never had heat except in the galley; and the galley fire didn't do us any good because ordinarily no one was allowed in there except the two cooks. It was so small they had mighty little elbow room anyway.

Some persons would have had their appetites spoiled by seeing the food prepared while the vessel rolled around and the slush accumulated on the floor. If pieces of food that got onto the floor were in the way, the cooks would kick them into corners so they wouldn't be stepped on. Besides, bags were put on the floor to modify its slipperiness.

Once or twice a day the cooks had the cadets swash out the galley and clean it up. It didn't smell, and it wasn't unwholesome. What I disliked most was to see a cook taste the soup and then wipe the spoon on his apron, which was so dirty you couldn't tell what color it was.

Our clothes didn't dry out unless we went to bed with them on, but even drying them like that was worth while because it was a great comfort in the morning to at least have dry clothes next to the skin. We were getting used to being cold now. I had become an expert at pulling in my neck when a sea swished over me so that less ice water would go down my back. When possible, I slanted arms and legs away from the rush of the water.

We all found it necessary to have a lashing around the waist to keep the sea from going up under our oilskin jackets, and more lashings were needed around wrists and ankles. The lashing around our waist, together with one which passed between our legs, and was fastened to the waist-lashing at front and back, was called "Body and soul lashing." Our buttons were continually snapping off and weren't dependable like lashings.

The second mate always was in the thick of things. He had to lead the gang and take the most responsible posts. No one got soaked so many times. Again and again he found his oilskins so useless that he took them off and chucked them into the chart room. He knew he wouldn't get any wetter without them, and their absence gave him much freer action.

"Did you see me swimming on the foredeck?"

he asked me one time. "There's so much water on that deck you can't walk—you *have* to swim."

During storms there was a lot of loafing-time, for the ordinary routine work of the ship couldn't be done. In the worst of the storms we just stood by waiting for things to happen, and ready to jump at a moment's notice.

The most strenuous periods were at the beginning of storms, taking in sail and lashing things to withstand the assaults of wind and sea, and at the end of storms setting sail and repairing damage. Some damage was done to the ship by any storm that blew more than fifty miles an hour. Officially, a fifty mile wind is rated as "a strong gale."

Tuesday night, for the first time in more than a week, we were on the proper course for two hours. There was a strong westerly wind next morning, and by carrying upper and lower tops'ls, fores'l, stays'ls, and spanker, we made about eight knots on the wind in a fairly rough sea. The royal yard was a fine place to stand on to get a view of the ship, water, and sky.

Our second mate frequently shook his head over the foolhardiness of the *Peking's* starting the voyage on Friday. It looked as if he were right, didn't it? But nothing affected the keenness of our appetite on Friday or any other day. Everything went, from raw herring to lard on our bread instead of butter.

While reading on Wednesday night, I heard the mate's whistle blow. Another gale had started and there was sail to be taken in.

I was rather cold, and in order to get warm I went out into the howling wind to help take in the upper tops'l. You have to fight every minute of the time while sail-furling in a gale. There is hanging on to be done as well as plenty of work at such a time, and the exercise is so strenuous you can't help but get warm.

One of the boys had his head split open by a sea that knocked him against something which was harder than his cranium. I watched the captain doctoring him. It made me mad to see the rough way he used a shaving-brush, a razor, and raw alcohol on his patient. If he were a horse-doctor I would hate to be a horse in his care.

But he wasn't wholly unqualified for his responsibility in connection with the ailing and maimed; for he had to have some medical knowledge and pass a test in order to get a captain's berth. His main dependence was a book of first aid information.

Thursday morning the wind was blowing in great shape. These German skippers hang onto sail just as long as possible, and that makes much harder the task of taking it in. Our fores'l was still set, and it was made of the heaviest canvas. The captain decided to take it in when noon came with more wind.

So all hands, except the first trip boys, were called, and amid tremendous shouting we hauled up the clew and buntlines from the deck where seas completely soaked us. Then forty of us swarmed up to the yard where we divided and slid out along the footropes, twenty on each side of the mast. There, shoulder to shoulder we clung to the yard and began furling the flapping sail, which was rumbling and cracking with a noise like thunder. Even with that gang working at the task it took a long time to furl the spray-wet sail. The ship then hove to with only lower tops'ls and a forestays'l set.

The gale kept increasing, and in the afternoon those North Sea waves were the biggest the captain ever had seen there. What else could we expect? This was our *thirteenth* day out of Hamburg. Some seas rolled us thirty-five degrees and knocked two lifeboats loose at one end, though they were double-lashed. Our radio aerial was blown away, and plenty of other damage was done.

Things certainly were in a mess down below. The gimbals of the big lamp in the captain's dining-saloon weren't rigged to swing far enough, and the metal-rimmed shade hit them with such a jar, that smash went the lamp chimney. The wild pitching of the vessel tipped a steaming pot of coffee down the steward's neck.

Several of the boys were kept busy bailing out rooms and passages, and even the captain's cabin hadn't escaped. Everything was sopping except the cargo. That was in the hold which was sealed practically water-tight.

Charlie and I had quite a problem to fix things so we could sleep with any comfort amid all the wetness in our cold, unheated room. His solution was to take off his oilskins and rubber boots, dungarees, jumper, and one sweater; and sleep in his pants, two pairs of underwear, two shirts, and two pairs of wet socks. Over these socks he pulled a sweater and stuck his feet in the armholes to encourage the socks to dry. The two ship's blankets and his own two were snugged around him, and his heavy outer sweater and other spare clothing capped the pile.

"It looks as if a hippopotamus had camped in your bunk," I remarked to him once, after he was comfortably settled.

"Yes," he said, "and I've noticed that's just how it looks in your bunk when you have your little mountain of bedclothes humped up."

For several weeks we went to bed with that

mess of things on us. It was the only way to dry them.

We were off Amsterdam that Thursday afternoon with a real west-northwest full gale blowing. This placed us on a very bad lee shore, and we couldn't do a thing to help ourselves in the tremendous seas that were driving us toward the land.

The captain thought he would try to anchor, but on inspection we found that the violent waves had heaved the two anchors up from where they were catted at the bow, and hooked them onto the deck. It was too rough to use the anchor davit to get them off, and we might as well have had no anchors at all.

By this time the radio aerial had been fixed, and a call sent out for tugs; but they wouldn't come except for salvage money, which meant half the value of the ship and cargo, and the captain wouldn't pay that. The storm was continually getting worse, and all the time the ship drifted toward land.

There was little for the crew to do. Two men

were at the wheel, and one man was stationed on the forward part of the midships deck as a lookout. The captain was on deck almost constantly and had been for the past two days. As a whole the crew just stood around in their oilskins, one gang up under the foc'sle head, and another gang near the steering gear underneath the poop deck.

I had been watching the storm from one place and another since eight o'clock in the morning, and what a wild and glorious sight it was—both beautiful and terrifying! This was the kind of storm I had wished for at the Giants Causeway.

About midnight we could see lights on the shore toward which we were drifting, and the captain radioed to the tugs to have them come anyway. I was in the chart room with him when the wireless operator came from his shack with their reply. The captain, after reading it, said, "Vell, dose tugs can't come. Der storm is too bad."

After a little figuring, which he did leaning over the chart table, he turned to me and said,

"If dis keeps up ve vill be driven ashore about six in der morning."

Friday the thirteenth had begun, and didn't we start on a Friday? So the captain was almost certain that our fate was sealed. While we were talking about this, a sea came over the side of the midship's deck and into the lee door of the chartroom and went on down the stairway.

Except for time taken to eat, I had been on deck sixteen hours. If we were going to be driven ashore it would be well to get some sleep so as to be better able to hang on to the rigging or swim.

Before I left the chart room I looked into the log book and saw that the captain had made a midnight entry estimating that the strength of the wind since six o'clock had been at force twelve, the highest rating in the Beaufort Scale, which describes Number Twelve as a hurricane. But now the wind was blowing more violently than ever. Plainly we were having a *first-class* hurricane.

I went below to turn in. A sister ship of the

Peking's was scheduled to sail in a couple of weeks for Valparaiso, and I decided that in case our ship were wrecked I would have to swim ashore and finish the voyage on that other ship.

So I went to sleep and let the skipper do the worrying. We all had confidence in his quality as a seaman and knew that he would stay on his job and do whatever could be done.

I slept well until about four o'clock, when I woke up with a queer feeling that something was wrong. The motion of the ship wasn't as it should be. She was rolling and pitching around as if she were in a ground swell near shore. The thought flashed into my mind that we were about to be wrecked, and that our shipmates in their confusion had forgotten to call us.

Up I got in a hurry and shook Charlie, shouting: "Get on deck quick! We're going to be wrecked!"

He seemed quite interested, but he didn't have much to say. In fact, we both put all our effort into getting our clothes on. We had crawled into our bunks without taking off anything but our

hip boots, sou'westers, and oilskins; and one
wouldn't think that dressing would be much of
a job. But we didn't want to take the time to
light our oil lamp, and the way the ship was
lurching we were not at all sure of lighting it
if we tried. So there we were struggling to get
dressed in darkness you could have cut with a
knife. Getting on the boots wasn't so bad. Most
of the trouble was with the oilskins. The linings
were wet and kept catching on the boots and the
several thicknesses of clothes we were wearing.
In that pitch-dark room, with the din of the
storm in our ears, and the vessel rolling crazily,
and both of us in a frantic hurry, every minute
seemed an hour.

Well, at last the final button was buttoned, the
final lashing tied, and our sou'westers were snapped on.

Then we groped along out to a stairway, and
still in darkness kept on up to the chart room
where there was a light. But we didn't stop. We
went out on the midships deck where the cold
flying spray, driven by the hurricane, cut our

faces. Here were the captain and two mates, and there were a couple of men at the wheel, three or four on lookout, and a few others standing by waiting to do whatever the skipper might order. Of course they all wore oilskins, and there they were, vague figures in a gloom that was only brightened by the little compass light.

I didn't dare speak to the skipper. He had been without sleep for three days and nights. All his thought was for the ship.

I was startled when he bent over the compass and its eerie little light shone up in his face. He looked haggard, worried, and old; his eyes were bloodshot, and he had a three-days growth of beard.

I spoke to the mate. "We've been drifting closer to land all the time," he told me, "and if there isn't a change pretty quick, we'll be wrecked all right."

Three lighthouses were in sight. Two of them were fairly near, and the mate said they were at the entrance to the North Sea Canal. It was surprising how calm and collected he and the

other seamen were in the face of such nearly
inescapable shipwreck.

A half hour or so passed and then unexpectedly, the wind began to moderate and to shift
gradually to the southwest. At that, what a hub-
bub there was on deck! Commands came thick
and fast, and all hands jumped to the braces to
wear ship.

Slowly she swung, heading more and more toward the land, because she only could swing her
bow away from the wind; we could see the tremendous, foaming, phosphorescent breakers
crashing over a reef between us and the lights on
shore. The *Peking* takes between two and three
miles to turn in, and there was scarcely more
than a three mile space between us and the reef.
Closer and closer she ran turning so slowly that
we had to watch the compass to make sure she
was swinging at all. She kept turning, and finally
we were headed out into the North Sea. Then,
by cracking on a lot of sail, we managed to get
away from the coast.

We kept setting sails from time to time the entire day, and by night all but the royals and a few stays'ls were hung out. The wind went down to a moderate southwesterly, which didn't do us much good, for there we were facing a head wind once more.

I said to Charlie, "Perhaps we will be North Sea pilots before we get out of here."

"Yes," he agreed glumly, "two old, gray-headed North Sea pilots."

The crew got out some two-and-one-half inch wire cable, and we started making a new top-mast stay to replace the broken one. If the masts had gone I suppose we would have rigged up the two big wooden spars that were lashed on deck reserved for emergencies.

Saturday we were exactly where we had been the previous Saturday. The fishing boats and lightships that had seen us around there for a couple of weeks must have thought we were out yachting, or sailing for our health.

We had fine sailing all day beating down in the general direction of Dover. It was a great sight to see the *Peking* come about. The crew

hauled the spanker amidships, let go the heads'l
sheets, put the helm down, and as soon as the
sails on the foremast were aback, the other yards
just ghosted around by themselves. Then the
foremast yards were pulled around by elbow-
grease applied to the brace winch.

When a ship of this size comes about in a
fresh breeze, your first impulse is to jump right
overboard. You can't imagine that the long
heavy steel yards could swing so fast without
breaking off and coming down on your head.
Meanwhile the brace winches, with a wild howl,
whirl so swiftly that the brakes are useless.

When we took our Sunday sights we were
within a few miles of our noon position twelve
days before. We had picked up a fair wind that
morning to push us through the English Channel, and in the middle of the day the wind was
supplemented by a tug which the owners of the
ship had sent out from Amsterdam, because they
had learned how close we had come to being
wrecked.

The tug captain reported, that in the worst

storm of the series that had assailed us, sixty-nine ships had been wrecked. Vessels had even been driven ashore right in Hamburg harbor. Not for half a century had there been so bad a storm in these waters.

I went to the chart room. There on the table lay the North Sea chart which we had been using so constantly for the past seventeen days. What a worn and weather-beaten thing it was after such a period of salt-water drippings from sou'westers and wet hands! The network of crisscross courses and noon positions marked on it looked more like a Chinese puzzle than the track of a respectable ship.

From winter to summer

IV

FROM WINTER TO SUMMER
ON THE ATLANTIC

Eᴀʀʟʏ on Monday, December 16th, we let the
tug go. Then for the first time we set all sail including the royals and the spanker gaff tops'l.
This made a total of thirty-one sails, and the
Peking was a wonderful sight.

She now had more than an acre of canvas
spread to the light northwesterly breeze which

shoved us along eight knots an hour. About noon a lingering haze lifted and gave us a look at the Isle of Wight with the sun shining on the houses and cliffs.

The captain knocked thunder out of two or three boys who didn't steer properly. One he slapped with his slipper. He often came on deck wearing slippers in good weather, and when irritated he occasionally pulled one off and used it for chastising purposes. A boy who was looking on with me at a slipper-slapping said, "Ven I see zee capatan, I travel a beeg circle so I vill not meet him."

That evening I spent several hours on deck. If land-dwellers could be on the *Peking* some such night with a full moon shining, and with a light following breeze, they would know why men go to sea on sailing ships.

I knew the name now of nearly every line on the vessel, and could obey orders given in German.

The weather continued to be fine on Tuesday and a very light air from aft ghosted us along at three knots. There was no swell to rattle things aloft, and no waves to splash at the sides, and nearly all the sails hung limp. The ship was as quiet as a graveyard.

Everybody was busy on board after the North Sea gales, when most types of industry were impossible. The iron worker and carpenter had gotten out the forge and repaired various iron fittings. The galley stovepipe, which in all vessels is called Charlie Noble, for some unknown reason, was getting rusty and was given a coat of paint, and much of the wire rigging was greased down.

The finest place from which to watch the sunset, was on the royal yard standing with my back against the mast. On such a day with very little wind and a smooth sea, I felt as I stood there that I might take a deep breath and fly.

But after a look down at the little men running around on the deck I decided that a tighter grip on the mast was desirable. In a storm, I liked to get up there and sing, because then I was sure no one would be bothered by the noise I made.

Wednesday we were on the port tack making about seven knots with twenty-nine sails set. We had the Lizard abeam at noon, though beyond sight, and were leaving the southwesternmost part of England behind and putting out to sea for good. During the afternoon we hoisted the anchors on deck, bolted them down, and stowed the chains below in the chain locker.

The chief mate was a small man thirty-nine years old, but he still could walk on his hands and do various stunts that he used to do when he was a boy. Often several of us got together when we had our half hour off for coffee in the afternoon, and each tried the stunts that the other fellows did.

Our second mate was only twenty-five, but he had a captain's ticket. One day he put the skipper's dog in the pen with the pigs. He was so full of mischief he just couldn't help entertaining himself that way.

One of the things we had rather often for din-

Furling the royals

Charlie (at right) and another lad who have been aloft tarring

Irving with a salt cod to be soaked for cooking

ner was sweet raisin soup. We would find all
kinds of things in our food—for instance, grape-
vine bark up to six inches long in the raisin soup,
rotten peas and sturdy looking bugs in the pea
soup, and various kinds of beans were brought
on in such condition that one did best not to talk
about them, think about them, nor even look at
them.

Sometimes we were served a prune soup, with
dough balls that would do good service as sink-
ers for fishing in a strong current. But the food,
whatever its failings, always tasted good to me,
and I ate great quantities of everything in sight.

Once when the captain and I were in the dining saloon, a boy who was making his first voyage came in to get a boil fixed up. He saw that
the captain had a hat on; so he kept his own on.
But the captain, at sight of the boy's hat, swiped
it off and nearly took along the boy's head.
While stamping on the hat he delivered a seagoing lecture to the poor lad.

Whenever the captain spoke, the crew trem-
bled in their boots. "I'm too rough," he told me.

"Dot is vhy der company vill not let me command a steamship, but I do not like dem steamships nohow."

Trouble started when any of the crew talked back to him. His hands would get into action with disastrous results, they were so heavy and he used them with such muscular vigor. When he was a boy he worked on a steamer for several months, and in telling me about it he said, "The mates, they vould hit me mit their foot, but I vould grab der foot and tip dose mates over."

So the officers soon stopped hitting him with their feet. But when he flared up at the boys on the *Peking* and knocked them around, he forgot how he felt at their age.

The captain's mongrel dog was about as mean tempered as they make 'em, and one day he bit a boy so badly that the captain had to attend to the wound. When the dog showed up in the cabin later, the captain grabbed him by the neck with his great hand, slapped him, and threw him out of the door. It seemed to me that the dog would take a piece out of all of us before the trip was over.

After sailing west all day Thursday until just before supper, rain began falling, a gloom like midnight settled down on us, and then the wind shifted and caught us aback. What a commotion there was for the next hour! No one could see a thing. Nevertheless sails had to be taken in, and the captain and mates hollered so loud that they couldn't be understood. Numerous things went wrong, but the squall wasn't particularly heavy, and no damage was done.

The next day we got within one hundred and twenty-five miles of Spain, and the captain thought this was too close. So we turned and headed back toward England to get more sea-room. Also, our skipper wanted to keep well out of the Bay of Biscay because it was a bad place for a sailingship to be caught in. Often the prevailing winds hold vessels in the bay for several weeks if they are dependent on sails.

There must have been a heavy gale somewhere in the North Atlantic, because we now started jumping into a big swell. This disgusted the skipper all the more, it followed so close on our delay in the North Sea where we spent seventeen days within two hundred miles of Hamburg. If the *Peking* made a slow passage the owners blamed the skipper; so he held onto all sail while she jumped and dove like a wild horse. The ship was driven nearly under water by the press of sail, and her main deck was full to the rails, yet the "Old Man" still hung onto the royals!

The wind increased, but the order to furl the royals didn't come until one huge swell covered the whole forward part of the ship as far back as the midships deck. The foc'sle head and both forward hatches were driven under thousands of tons of water that stopped the ship dead. Her bow soon shook itself free, and then taking in sail began.

Several experienced hands were sent aloft to furl the royals which were snapping about as the ship plunged on. I thought I could hold on as well as the next man and I went with them. Out on the yards, standing on a swaying footrope, while the yards themselves were whipping around, I couldn't see how we were going to furl that sail, and at the same time hold on tight enough.

But the others started work just as the ship took a deep dive. The yard went forward with a snap that tore the fellow beside me right off the yard. Down he went.

Hardly had this happened when a wave under the bow brought the yard back just as quickly as it had gone. The fellow who dropped saw it returning just in time to catch hold of the foot rope where he had been standing, and soon he had pulled himself up on the yard, where with a smile at me, he went on furling the royal.

That is what experience on a sailing ship teaches—"Work for the ship while there is life left in your body."

Before coming down we furled not only the royals but the upper and lower to'gan's'ls. When the captain found out what I had been doing he said: "You should not have gone up there. It was too dangerous."

Our sailmaker could read English, and I lent him a couple of Morgan Robertson's salt water novels. He said that after reading some of the stories he saw rats and mad dogs in his sleep.

My own reading was mainly "The Outline of History" by H. G. Wells, and I found it quite interesting. The different parts of the world meant much more than names after seeing what I had in my wanderings. I wished that when going to high school I had wanted to know as many things as I wanted to know now. Charlie got out "The Ancient Mariner" once in a while and read parts of it aloud.

It was something that seemed to him to have just the atmosphere which fitted our circumstances; and I don't know how many times he said to me as he closed the book after a reading. "Boy, that's a great poem!"

Studying German took some of our attention right along, and we were entertained to find that the German word for gloves was "handshoes." You get a good many odd combinations like that in the language.

Our evening light was the big kerosene lamp that we shared with the captain in the dining saloon. Taking care of it was the steward's business, but he wasn't very dependable. Neither was the lamp. Sometimes water got into the kerosene and made the light go out, and sometimes it was so poorly trimmed that the captain would get the steward up out of bed to fix it. The fellow would come in mumbling, and heavy-eyed and mournful-looking, and that always made the captain laugh.

The big swell was still heaving us Saturday morning. How the vessel did slat and bang, with the yards braced hard up and the swell abeam! Presently the wind started to blow from the northwest and increased to a strong breeze with squalls of gale force. The captain was carrying a press of sail to drive the ship off shore, and she gave us plenty of action as she dove head on into the swells.

I got quite a knock while furling the mains'l. The wind caught it in such a way that a big iron clew ring was brought down on my head. It happened to hit a tough spot or I would have fallen off the yard.

When below deck, the creaking and laboring of the ship were rather ominous, but as the *Peking* was built for rounding Cape Horn I thought this noise must be her own little song.

It was three weeks since we left the Elbe, and we hadn't yet had a good breeze aft. I started a square-knot-belt for Charlie, and another for the sailmaker. So, with sail-making, splicing, helping the sailors up aloft, and doing athletic stunts, I found plenty to do.

I could trim them all at the stunts. I trimmed them, too, at splicing. That was because I had been taught by the head rigger at Herreshoffs, one of the most expert in America. Not a man on board could splice wire better than I did, or as fast.

Sunday night we passed a steamer that couldn't make anything like the *Peking's* speed in the big sea which both were wallowing in.

"We're running right away from her," Charlie said.

And I added, "This old windjammer is going to do some piling along if ever we get the right kind of wind."

"I'm getting to like her more and more," was Charlie's comment. "I guess I have fallen in love with her; but just the same I'd like to have solid ground under my feet for a while."

Tuesday, December 24th, the biggest news of the day was that I had shaved!

This was the first time I had used my razor since leaving Hamburg, twenty-eight days before; so I had gotten to look like a real deep sea sailor. Charlie gazed at me approvingly.

"Very good," he said, and then after a moment's pause remarked: "But your hair looks as wild as your whiskers did. Better let me trim it."

"All right, go ahead," I told him, and he soon was snipping away.

The locks of hair still were falling this way and that when my barber stopped work. He went on a strike, so to speak, saying, "I'll finish tomorrow when there's more light."

I gazed at myself in a pocket mirror, and

wasn't at all pleased with his handiwork. "This is no way to leave me," I grumbled. "You've made me look like an old moulting hen."

"Well," he said, "if you don't like your looks stow that mirror away." And that was all I could get out of him.

Christmas was at hand. The Germans make a great deal of it, and the ship owners had provided five Christmas trees and plenty of trimmings for them—also apples, nuts, dried bananas, and cookies for everyone on board. I helped count and divide the stuff, including two thousand cookies. The night before Christmas is the time the Germans celebrate most, although they have Christmas and the day after for legal holidays.

That evening all the boys went into one of their mess rooms where they had made preparations for a good time by trimming up two Christmas trees and lighting them with candles. As the ship heaved up and down, the branches of the trees lifted and dropped as if an erratic wind were blowing them.

Two of the boys had violins and two had ac-
cordions. They played very well, and the other
boys all sang. When the captain came in they
stood up and sang Christmas carols. Most of
them had presents from home, usually in the
form of food, which they passed out to me until
I couldn't eat another thing.

There was something about the bunch of boys
that evening, and the occasion, which made me
catch my breath. They were in a sort of trance
thinking of home and things far off in their na-
tive land. One wouldn't believe, to see them then,
that they could wrestle with a thrashing sail in
a storm.

On the 25th Charlie and I talked of home a
lot and made guesses as to what the folks were
doing at various times. The *Peking* was running
before a good wind on the course for the first
time that trip, and a big North Atlantic swell
abeam rolled us like a barrel.

I cut Charlie's hair, and did a fine job, if I do
say so—much better, I told him, than he de-
served after the way he left mine. The captain

volunteered to finish the clipping that Charlie had begun, and he did it very expertly, though handicapped in using the shears by the bigness of his fingers, which he could hardly get into the handle holes.

Our skipper just couldn't keep his hands off the shears whenever there was hair-cutting going on. One time I watched while he sneaked up on a boy who had long hair, and he was clipping it off before the poor fellow knew what was going on.

The candied fruit and other things sent to us at Hamburg from home were shared with our sea-faring friends, except the fruit cake. I was saving that for off Cape Horn.

The captain was superstitious about whistling. He thought it was a bad-weather breeder, and that it might cause the wrecking of the ship. He yanked a handful of hair out of the head of one boy who was whistling, and made him do penance for two hours on the royal.

Christmas Day was the first one of the voyage

when we could dry our clothes except by going to bed with them on.

A fresh northeasterly breeze was behind us on the 26th, and we had glorious sailing through clear, blue, sparkling water, with silver wave-tops. Such was the charm of the water that Charlie and I agreed we would like to jump in and sport about in it. The mate was close by on duty, and I called his attention to the nice clear water—so different from what we passed through in the North Sea.

Ten seconds afterward a wave of that crystal water scaled the midships deck and cracked me on the back, soaking me from head to foot. It didn't show the least appreciation of the complimentary things I'd been saying, but quite the opposite. No other wave for hours before had dashed up on the deck, nor did any other wave behave like that for hours afterward.

We passed the Canary Islands Friday morning at a distance of about twenty miles, and could have seen the tops of their mountains if they had not been hidden by clouds. All day the vessel sped along at a great rate, and we had what I call wonderful sailing. The great, frosted, blue seas came up from astern and shoved us ahead, and the water that was bowled along by the bow sometimes shot on past the end of our fifty-foot jib boom.

The next evening we crossed the tropic of Cancer, and on ahead of us lay over three thousand miles of sailing in the tropics. Just then we were stepping along at twelve knots, and weirdly impressive lightning was flashing around. It was a great sight to see our old wind bag hurrying through the seas, spreading them this way and that. Why does any one travel on a steamer except persons in a great hurry?

Sunday we were having the finest weather of our trip and could keep the portholes of our room open. It was so warm that most of the boys had stopped wearing shirts, and some went barefoot. The captain held a class in splicing for the first and second trippers, in spite of the fact that they weren't supposed to work on that day. Each boy took a short piece of rope and tried making the various kinds of splices.

For two or three days the crew were kept busy taking down, overhauling, oiling, and re-lashing the foot ropes that we used when we went out along a yard.

A sailing vessel takes the prize for hard usage of one's hands. Mine were not in as bad shape as those of most of the horny-handed crew, because I didn't do as much dirty work, like tarring down, for instance. When hauling on the lines and handling the sails, especially in cold weather, our hands got badly cracked and cut. We couldn't wash very clean, fresh water was so scarce, and most of us had infected fingers or wrists.

New Year's Day was celebrated by omitting work. However, the mates gave the first trippers a rope chase. A mate would call out the name of some line, and the boys had to run to catch hold of that line. If they didn't go fast enough they got a kick, or a swat with a rope's end. In their haste they banged into each other, fell down, or went to the wrong places.

There was a mad scramble early in the morning when we had a lifeboat drill. Two boats were swung out, one on each side.

The sailmaker made a canvas coat for himself, and painted it so it would serve as an oilskin. Actual use proved it to be the best waterproof coat on board. Another thing he made out of canvas was first-class seaboots for himself and the officers.

There were plenty of flying fish about now, and a cadet took one that landed on the foredeck, tacked it on a flat board with the long wing-like fins spread out, and put it in the sun to dry. He was going to take it home as a souvenir.

The next day was fine and warm, "flying fish weather" sailors call it, and we started making a new cro'jack sail on deck. It was to be over ninety feet wide and thirty-three feet high.

One thing that we had for dinner was a sweet soup made of raisins, currants, prunes, pork, apples, salt horse, pears, sugar, bacon, vinegar,

gooseberries, spices, and barley. All the fruits
were dried, and they mostly came from Cali-
fornia. Our bacon usually was served without
frying, and was so tough that it could hardly be
cut. The cold boiled potatoes were drowned in
vinegar before we got a chance at them. This
made them much sharper than I relished.

Another item in our bill of fare that I wasn't
enthusiastic about was pickled pork. Imagine a
dish of cold pork that was just a sickly white
mass of fat surrounded by brine, and jiggling
like gelatine. The only way we could get even
a little of it down was to mix it with plenty of
potato.

The hard black bread was our standby, and
we ate it in preference to white bread. It always
was kept several weeks to harden after it was
baked, so we wouldn't eat it too freely. A sailor
took a piece of that black bread and hit a wooden
door with the edge of it. Quite a dent was made
in the door, but the bread wasn't damaged. The
captain drank fifteen to twenty cups of coffee

every day, and the second mate got away with three or four bottles of beer.

While up on the royal on a quiet evening I whistled all the tunes I could remember, not thinking that the whistling could be heard on deck. Later Charlie told me that the sailors heard me plainly, like a bird in a tree. One tune I whistled was "America" which was taboo in Germany because their words that go with it mean, "Hurrah for the Kaiser!"

The sunset and cloud formations as I saw them that evening from the royal were wonderful. There were more freaks of light, clouds, and color than I ever had seen before in one day. I wished some one could enjoy the sight with me, but perhaps the sense of loneliness made it more appealing.

One morning when I was taking a trick at the wheel, I hardly had begun my steering when the wind hauled two points ahead so we had to go off the course. The captain was sure I was a Jonah after that. Before I got through, the wind went down almost to a calm. We had just enough for steerage way, but not enough to keep the sails from slatting.

The mate shot a dolphin with his pistol, but of course he couldn't get it. So he went to the sail-making room and got a harpoon to keep at the bow ready for any other dolphins that might come along.

In the doldrums with flapping sails and no wind

V

OUT OF THE DOLDRUMS AND DOWN TO THE HORN

THE *Peking* was getting into the doldrums—that listless strip of the Atlantic just north of the equator, which stretches across to Africa from nearly opposite the mouth of the Amazon. Unsettled weather prevails there, with short squalls, and calms, or winds that are light and baffling.

On two days we were slowed down to an average speed of scarcely more than a mile an hour, and there was plenty of hauling on the braces to take advantage of whatever puffs came along. The *Peking,* on her preceding voyage, had slatted around in the doldrums for a fortnight before she could get through its two or three hundred miles width.

Here we had our first real rain after getting into warm weather. A regular doldrum downpour started in, and we hurriedly swept off the midships deck, set buckets under the pipes that let the water run to the lower decks, and as fast as the buckets filled carried them to a couple of big steel tanks, one on the fore deck, and one on the after deck. Those held our water for washing. Incidentally the boys had some fun throwing bucketsful over each other.

The next day was quiet and sunny and half the crew were busy washing their clothes and hanging them to dry on lines that they stretched in the rigging. Everybody on the vessel was his own washerman, including the captain, who indeed was the most expert scrubber of any of us.

But why shouldn't he be? He had had forty years of practice at it.

Charlie, who couldn't seem to concentrate his mind enough on the washing to do it well, held up a sample for my inspection, saying: "I wish the skipper would do this washing for me. He gets the clothes cleaner than any one else, yet doesn't wear them out."

"Then why don't you ask him to do yours?" I suggested.

"Say! I'd rather die a natural death," was his answer.

Clothes-washing was out of the question while crossing the North Sea, or rounding the Horn, on account of storms and cold. Our laundry weather was limited to about a month in the middle of the trip.

Charlie and I had more washing to do than any of the rest of the crew except the officers, because we each had a sheet on our beds and the others didn't. If the sheets were going to be washed we must do it ourselves. So we went at them, but not with any spirit. Laundrying wasn't a job that appealed to either of us, and that was the one and only washing the sheets got during the trip.

One thing that we congratulated ourselves on was an absence of vermin. There were no signs of any close neighbors, except that cockroaches were plentiful in the galley. But I had seen them a whole lot thicker in regular passenger ships.

Sunday, the 5th, one of the men caught a fine bonito, and in less than two hours we were eating it—a welcome break in the salt horse diet. It was two or three feet long, bluish in color, and had narrow, slanting, black stripes on its upper part. Skipjack is another name for it.

To catch this kind of fish, a piece of white cloth was tied to a hook and jumped along the top of the water under the jib boom. The bonito thought the cloth was a flying fish and leaped for it.

The captain, aided by the chief mate and carpenter, gave the dog a bath. It was a good show for the onlookers. After soaking him properly the captain nearly drowned him in a barrel of salt water. That roused the wrath of the dog, and when he was let loose there was a great scramble to get out of his way.

In the early weeks of our voyage, while knocking around in the North Sea, we had our hands full contending with the storms. No attention was paid to Sunday, or, for that matter, to any other day, except Friday, which seemed to have some fateful connection with what had happened to us, and with what was going to happen to us.

But now things were fairly normal, and Sunday was recognized by not requiring the crew to do any more work than was necessary for the running of the ship. A good many of them slept in their leisure, and some did a little reading or mended their clothes. Others might do athletic stunts or sit around discussing prize fights and other sporting events. Often, when the weather was good, the crew's orchestra of about eight instruments would get out on deck to play while the rest of the fellows sang.

Since leaving the English Channel a regular

feature of Sunday had been a rope chase for the first-trippers. The second or third mate had charge of it, and the chase lasted an hour or more. Many times the boys were kept running during the night watches. It was a part of the boy's education, and was work, not recreation. It taught the boys the ropes—that is, the names and positions of all the several hundred lines used in handling the ship.

When the mate with his stinging rope's end got tired of whacking them he sent them up to some line at the masthead while he rested his arm; and when he got tired of chasing them around the deck he would set the skipper's dog after them to keep them running. The dog's biting wasn't merely playful. He put his teeth right into their flesh!

Most of the older men smoked pipes, and the cadets usually smoked cigarets. Tobacco was costly, and they made weekly vows not to buy so much of it next Sunday from the slop chest.

There was practically no drinking. Only once was any grog passed out. That was in a bad storm, and none but the older men got it. The captain didn't approve of drinking for young fellows. Two of the mates had their beer, and our skipper drank wine, but made a single bottle last through the trip.

Monday, January 6th, we got plenty of showers, but no wind. Our deck tanks were full of fresh water, and between showers nearly all of us hung out some washing that we were trying to get dry.

I fished for bonito one morning until the captain told me to get off the end of the jib boom because I was the Jonah that was making the calm.

We had a big dragnet that was towed along by a rope tied to the tip of the jib boom. It caught tropical surface sea-life which was to go to a German museum. The net was so constructed that it captured creatures no larger than a pinhead, and from that up to those a foot long. They were all shapes and colors, and some were the queerest things imaginable.

The captain had a special glass that magnified

Repairing sails

Irving Johnson with a spear after bonito

the smaller specimens. He kept them in bottles of preservative. Nothing was paid by the museum, but if the captain found a new species he was rewarded by having it named after him.

We caught a jelly-fish called Venus's girdle. It was a foot or so long, thin and narrow like a belt, and transparent except for a very slight bone structure. The head was about the size of a match head, and mostly consisted of two blue eyes and a small mouth.

Another interesting jelly-fish, and one that we saw in great numbers, was the Portuguese man-of-war. They could blow up a blue, purple, or pink bladder and float on the surface so that the breezes wafted them along. The crew called them "by-the-winders" because of their likeness to a ship sailing by the wind. They seemed to have a fine time voyaging around on the ocean.

For breakfast we sometimes had golden mackerel that were caught the same morning. They tasted even better than bonito. Often our jib boom looked like a henroost with all the fishermen and fishermen's advisers out on it.

Seven mackerel were caught with hook and line, or with the fish spear one day. They were about two and a half feet long and weighed fifteen to twenty pounds each. I would just as soon have stayed in the doldrums a couple of weeks, it was such sport trying to spear fish that came to the surface right under the jib boom.

On the 8th we were in the south-east trade winds and had fair weather all day. Sailing ships conserve their water supply by making it difficult to get at. Our big deck tanks had only a two inch hole in the top, and through that we had to get the water by dangling down a little can on a string. This sort of water conservation is the limit of inconvenience, and thereby, I suppose, achieves its purposes. Naturally, we sailors unexpectedly found a half bucket of the water drawn up through that little hole sufficient to wash a great quantity of clothes.

We had cheese rind in the soup one day, and on the day after that dried cherry soup in which we put rice and zweibeck. It tasted very good. Also, on occasion, we were served blueberry

Dipping water out of the deck tank through a two inch hole

Collecting rainwater for washing clothes

Our orchestra

soup, which was another variety I never had
heard of before.

We crossed the equator Thursday afternoon,
and all the crew, except those cadets who were
first trippers, were eager to have a visit from
King Neptune. But the captain wouldn't allow
the old fellow on board. He said that Neptune
and his court were so rough, that they often
made trouble which had to be settled in the
courts after the ship got back to Germany.

The sail maker was more disappointed than
any one else by this banning of Neptune. He
had some paraphernalia all ready in the sail
room, and showed it to me. "See," he said, and
held aloft a fish spear. "Dis is Neptune's trident,
and here is his mask mit der long vhiskers, and
look! Here is his wooden razor for shaving der
greenhorns."

A lot of bonito kept us company under the
bow nearly all day, but no one had the luck to
catch any. They weren't hungry enough to take
a hook and were too quick to spear.

The crew overhauled all the buntlines and

clew garnets. Each of these was unrove, repaired, and greased on deck. To put them back a man had to go down from the yard in a bo'son's chair to the foot of the sail, where he dangled until he made them fast.

The carpenter constructed a devil's fiddle which added a new note to our evening band-and-singing concerts. Its main features were a holystone stick with a small tin pan fastened flat against it about a foot from the bottom. Over the pan, up along the stick, were strung three light flexible wires, and on each wire were threaded about twenty small pieces of tin the size of a thumb nail, but of various shapes. On the top of the stick three round pieces of tin four inches or so in diameter were loosely held by a single nail through their centers. The bow was a flat stick a couple of feet long, with numerous shallow notches cut in the edge.

When in use, this devilish contraption was held something like a base viol, with its lower end resting on the deck. The musician sawed back and forth across the wires, and once in a

while bounced the whole thing on the deck to
make the pieces of tin clatter. The noise was
surprisingly agreeable in connection with the
rest of the music. It wasn't inharmonious. We
liked it, and there was humor in the looks of the
instrument and the method of playing it.

The sailmaker supplied two other queer sea
music makers. One was a big drum made of
canvas nicely stretched over a sugar keg. The
other was a fine steel marline spike about a foot
and a half long with a string hitched to it. He
played it himself, by simply taking the end of
the string in one hand and holding the marline
spike suspended, while he hit it with a stick held
in his other hand. Thus he brought forth pleasant
ringing tones that had a good deal of charm.

We were only one hundred and fifty miles
due east from Pernambuco, Brazil, on Monday,
the 13th. I did a lot of necessary repairing on my
one good suit and then sponged it off. While
repairing my dungarees with some old cloth of
the captain's that I hadn't asked him for, he
came along and picked up a piece.

"Well," I said, putting on a bold front, "did you ever see that before?"

"Oh, yes," he said. "I had a suit made of it in 1911. Fine cloth!"

The royal was a good place for dreaming in the evening, but there was danger of forgetting to hold on, or of going to sleep. The dreaming arrangements were not all they ought to have been, with only the yard to stand or sit on. On a nice night, after I had forgotten the fight with gravity getting up there, and had taken a look at the moon and stars and at the phosphorescent lights in the water caused by fish, it seemed as if I didn't have to hold on, but could walk out on the air.

We had made fast time since leaving the Lizard, in spite of being slowed down a few days in the doldrums. There was some prospect of our overcoming even the handicap of being held so long buffetted by the gales in the North Sea.

The crew seemed to be having a spell of dropping such things as marline spikes, hammers,

Caulking the hatches for rounding the Horn

Sorting potatoes

and bolts from where they were at work on the yards. Many of these articles fell into the sea, but some landed on deck and raised howls of reproof from the captain and mates.

Tuesday we saw a big two-stack steamship heading north about five miles away.

I wrestled with one of the crew on the fore-hatch and got rather scratched up, but he fared worse than I did in the wrestling.

Off Argentina the hatch tarpaulins were removed, and the hatch covers calked with oakum in preparation for Cape Horn. The captain figured how many voyages he had made around the Cape. The one he was making was his fifty-second. No other man has made the trip around the Horn as many times as that. He had been with this same ship company, and on the same run, ever since he started going to sea.

One of the boys who was steering forgot which way to turn the wheel, and got all the sails aback —that is, with the wind on the wrong side. The captain was angry, and he threw the boy out of the way like a sack of meal and had some one else take his place.

The boys sorted over our tons of potatoes, and took out the rotten ones. And while they were about it they made a bad mess throwing the rotten ones around—mostly at each other. If a fellow got smacked with one, he always tried to send back another that was bigger and juicier and hurled with more vigor.

The radio operator who had charge of the stores was at his wit's end, for the boys did pretty much as they pleased no matter what he said. Finally the captain got wind of what was going on. A little overseeing on his part ended the ructions, and the boys sorted more potatoes in an hour than they had before in a day.

Every once in a while Charlie and I got out my Christmas fruit cake to smell of it. We thought of home and of the delicious feast that cake was going to furnish us before long.

At noon on Friday, the 16th, we were almost vertically under the sun. Our shadows were gone, and even the big sails cast none worth mentioning. The wooden deck got too hot to stand on with bare feet, and we either wore shoes, or made quick runs from one narrow shadow to another, pausing on each in turn.

We didn't eat nearly as much as we did where the weather was cold.

The crew started scraping rust spots and red-leading them. It was the first painting they had done this trip. I could sew canvas fairly well by this time because I had been at it right along.

Some weeks previous, Charlie and I had started walking on our hands and doing tumbling stunts in our spare time. This got the whole crew started, and now it was a regular circus to see them.

We had gotten out of the southeast trades, and had a light northerly breeze. I did my first steering before the wind, and it was fairly easy if I kept constant watch of the compass, but several times I let the ship get off the course and had quite a job getting her back. The officers expected whoever was steering not to let her get off the course more than a quarter of a point.

January 20th the weather changed to a cool rain with a variable wind, and the whole gang ran around in the rain without much on and filled the deck tanks again.

A big shark was caught on the stout shark hook, but it shook itself off before we could slip a noose onto it. The captain towed a one inch hook with a rag on it nearly all day, and he caught a beautiful golden mackerel that evening. It was so heavy, that if he had tried hauling it out with a line the hook would have broken. Instead he used the fish spear, and after four throws got the mackerel. It was well over three feet long and weighed twenty-eight pounds.

A fine sunset turned the whole sky, sea, and ship a brilliant red. What a wonderful sight!

Nearly all the next day a brown shark followed us, but it wouldn't do more than nibble the meat on the hook that we towed at the stern. I didn't blame the shark for not taking that bait, for it was the same pickled pork which was served to *us*.

There must have been over a hundred pilot

fish along with the shark, and if they attended properly to the piloting there was small chance that the shark ever would run aground. They were a foot or so long, amber colored, and broadly banded. Their name was given them by sailors, who so often saw them swimming with a shark, that they imagined the fish really acted as pilots.

Once the shark came so close that the captain let drive his harpoon at it, but the harpoon opened before striking, so the iron didn't penetrate at all. After that the shark stayed farther back, while the boys tried unsuccessfully to catch pilot fish with bent pins they put on their lines.

The following morning a six-foot shark was caught, and the sailors cut out the big liver and let the sun try out the oil. This they would use later to rub on their hands. The captain claimed it was the best ointment in the world to keep cold, wet, and stiff hands from cracking. One boy saved the flippers, another the tail, another the jaws and teeth, and still another treasured the pupils of the eye which would harden like rock and make good cuff links.

Later we heard the call of "swine fish" at the bow, and there was a scramble to see them. What we saw was several dolphins sporting in and out of the water and grunting in a way that made clear how they got the "swine fish" name. The captain harpooned one, but the dolphin bent and broke the heavy iron harpoon and escaped.

We started overhauling the life boats, which always is an interesting job. The forge was out on deck every day, and was kept busy repairing various iron fittings and making new cargo hooks.

Thursday, the 23rd, we picked up a fine easterly breeze on the quarter. The weather was cooler now, but we still didn't need to wear a shirt in the daytime.

The next day we made one hundred miles from noon to eight o'clock in the evening with a fine breeze two points abaft the beam. The old *Peking* gave us quite a show charging through the water at this speed.

The idea of economy on the ship was to save every piece of string, wire, or rope over six inches long. Even canvas parceling nearly twenty years old had been saved. I never had seen anything to equal this saving mania. Of course it was a tremendous waste of the men's time, but that is the last thing they think of saving on sailing ships.

Saturday we made nearly twelve knots an hour for the whole day, that is, 281 miles, the longest noon to noon run on the voyage. Few freighters can beat that. We were off the mouth of the River Plate—a vicinity noted for storms, squalls, pamperos, and weather freaks of all kinds, and it seemed to me that during the night we got samples of every one of them.

The crew had been busy for several days putting chafing gear on some large new cane baskets that were to be used for handling certain kinds of cargo, such as coke. They wired barrel staves all around the sides, and wound old rope around the top and bottom edges. The strengthening of each basket required the work of two men for over a week.

The captain had a strange sense of humor. His greatest sport was to sic the dog on to me. The dog had bitten me twice, but now I was an expert at fighting him off with my bare hands.

Charlie cut my hair again one day. Then I cut his, and unfortunately nipped his ear. "Gee, Charlie!" I said, "I didn't intend to do that. I'm sorry."

His comeback was: "Oh! go ahead. I have another ear."

Anyhow, it was the lurching of the ship that caused the mishap.

Whole schools of fish about two feet long swam this way and that near the ship as if on a cruise. They wouldn't touch a hook, and were too quick to spear. Several sea lions played around just out of reach of the harpoon.

One evening we passed a four-mast tops'l schooner about ten miles off.

I was getting so I liked curry and rice, and I knew how to make away with salt horse in good shape since learning to cut it up fine and mix it well with potato.

For some time the Southern Cross had been within view in the night sky. It's a punk cross and not easily recognized. The four stars are far from being evenly bright and one is decidedly dim. As a constellation it can't compare with the Great Dipper or Orion. You don't realize it is a cross until it is pointed out to you. The sailors speak of the Cross as pointing to the South Pole, and if you draw a line through the two brightest stars that is where it points.

We had passed through what is known as "the silver stream" off the River Plate. It is the river water not yet mixed with the sea, and that silvery tone is imparted by the dirt in solution. After getting beyond it, the sea was a fine, clear, light green.

Wednesday, the 29th, we made fourteen knots from eight to nine in the morning. This was a lucky day because of the feed we got at noon. I had all the turkey, potatoes, gravy, and canned greens I could eat. On top of that I jammed three fourths of a prune pie. Such a chance wasn't apt to come more than once in a voyage, and it wouldn't have come when it did if the turkey hadn't got sick.

What a surprise—another feast next day! This time a sick hen had been discovered, and again unusual delicacies were served—chicken broth with rice, then chicken, potatoes, and creamed asparagus tips, and the feast was topped off with plum duff and prune sauce! The hens were laying a half dozen or more eggs a day; so on Sundays we each got two fried eggs for breakfast.

We stretched the new cro'-jack along the deck and seized on the reef rope. It was a tremendous sail, and we had been twenty-eight days making it. An average of four men had worked on the job eight hours a day. We estimated that the sail weighed nearly a ton.

We saw a large whale some distance away that evening. Albatrosses were keeping us company now, and the weather was so calm that they were obliged to work their wings some to stay up. If they rested on the water they had quite a job to

The new cro'jack

Some queer seaweed

get started off from it, and would go for a long distance hitting the water with their feet and making a chuck, chuck, chuck noise, meanwhile increasing their speed, until they left the surface. We had an escort of twenty or so of the big birds.

The captain knocked the breath out of one of the cadets, and then gave him the rope's end for poor splicing. It wasn't uncommon for the captain or mates to hit the boys with the end of a rope when they didn't do things right. The method was pretty savage, and no doubt something less brutal would have served, but it made the boys more efficient and thorough than would any amount of scolding.

One thing our skipper did was to put a stop to the boys' playing on their instruments or singing after eight o'clock at night because the music made the dog bark, and then his master couldn't sleep. A cadet made the comment that the captain liked to act the Kaiser, which was true.

He was a regular child in his way of saying or doing just the opposite of what any one else said or did. In his opinion everything should be done *his* way and anything he had was good, and anything you had was poor.

But whatever his failings he was a very expert skipper. If he was rough in his discipline, it was to get results, but he used less and less as the voyage progressed, because the cadets had become more efficient and didn't need it. Probably he never would have survived so many roundings of the Horn, had he not seen to it that the crew did their work perfectly.

One day he said to me: "Vot do dose poys call me? I know they call me 'The Old Man;' but maybe other times something much worse, hey?"

"Well, they're not very complimentary after you've been treating them rough," I acknowledged; "but among themselves it's mostly 'The Old Man,' that they call you. If anyone else is within hearing they say, 'The Captain'."

Early on the morning of the 31st, a German motor ship circled us. She was taking back to Germany some tourists who had been wrecked

on a vessel of the same line in a channel south
of the Strait of Magellan.

Our crew started rigging life lines on the foredeck; also overhauling life nets. This looked as
if serious business were not far away. The
strongest suit of sails was bent, and these sails
were made to stand up to quite a breeze.

The next day was Saturday, the 1st of February. There was little need for life lines this
morning, for we had no wind at all. We dipped
over the side of the ship with our long-handled
net and caught various types of sea-life including seaweed that had queer parasites feeding
on it. The seaweed that we pulled aboard made
a great heap. It would have filled six or eight
bushel baskets. There must have been at least
fifty different kinds of bugs living in it, and they
were all colors, sizes, and shapes.

Charlie came below in the evening, and as he
was passing the skipper's dog, the dog growled.
Charlie stopped to pet the dog, and without
warning, the unmannerly beast took a piece out
of the center of Charlie's palm. That was such

a surprise to Charlie he couldn't think of anything to say or do at first.

When he regained his voice, he said to the dog, "Well, you nut!" and turned to me with, "Did you ever see such a crazy dog?"

His hand had to be bandaged for some time before the wound healed and the soreness was out of it.

Saturday night we bowled along at fourteen knots for a couple of hours, but most of Sunday was calm. The wind had changed frequently and quickly in the last three days.

We tried to catch some albatrosses with a queer contrivance on a string prepared for the purpose. This was a piece of wood, to which was attached a V shaped strip of tin baited with meat. When an albatross picked at the meat, its hooked bill caught on the inside of the tin. Then the bird could be hauled in without harming it. One had been caught last trip whose wings had a spread of fifteen feet, and its head was large enough to just fit a boy's cap.

A Cape Horn ripsnorter

VI

TWO CAPE HORN RIP-SNORTERS

F ROM latitude fifty on the east of South America to latitude fifty on the West is called "the Horn," and mariners always figure from these points the number of days around. The distance as we planned to sail, going south of the Strait of Magellan and well away from the coast, was nearly a thousand miles. We crossed latitude fifty in almost a dead calm without a ripple on the water.

Many giant white jelly fish were adrift that would each fill a five bushel basket, and that had tails fifteen feet long. I spent four hours or more Monday, February 3d, on the royal looking down into the clear, quiet water at the schools of jelly-fish, some of them blobs of pulp, white, yellow, or brown, and some of them like long, filmy rubber ropes.

There were several kinds of sea birds that we had in sight frequently now. One was a combination creature, the penguin. It had hair like a dog, made a noise like a gull, looked like a duck when on top of the water, and like a seal when it was under water. It used its small wings swimming under water just as a bird would for flying in the air. Several that I was watching had a squabble over something or other, and one of them got mad and set out for distant parts in a hurry. For every two feet under water he would jump six feet out of water, and he made great

speed as far as I could see him, never stopping
to look back.

Monday, toward midnight, the captain came
into the room where Charlie and I were sound
asleep, and shook us, saying in an excited voice:
"Get up, get up! Der is something funny on der
sea. Come and look quick!"

So we piled out on deck. There was practically no wind, and the water was as smooth as
glass. "See!" the captain said, pointing to some
glowing phosphorescent streaks not far away in
the water. "Vot is it?"

The ship lazily moved closer, and we heard a
chipping noise that came from the surface of
the water. By this time the crew were hanging
over the rails gazing and listening wonderingly.
The glowing streaks through which the vessel
now was slowly gliding were five or six feet wide
and extended beyond our sight into the black
night. Between the streaks was open water with
an average breadth of thirty yards.

One of the sailors brought a handnet. It was
only a foot across, but had a handle twelve feet

or more long. The sailor perched himself on the rail, and aided by the fourth mate carefully dipped into the puzzling phosphorescence. Then they swung the net up on deck, and all of us jumped away, startled by the strange scraping noise that came from it.

Some one got a flashlight, and there we saw that the net was full of young lobsters about four inches long. These were dumped on the deck and the net was dipped down for more, while several of the boys went for washtubs to hold the prospective catch. The vessel drifted along for a couple of hours before we left the glowing streaks of floating lobsters behind. We had filled four tubs with them.

I went below in the middle of the affair to put on more clothes. Then, for my own entertainment, I stuck my head out of a port hole and made a low screeching noise. At once there was a rustle of excitement up above. The crew thought something else, mysterious, and perhaps dangerous, was at hand.

They stretched out over the rail to look, exclaiming in low, agitated voices, "Vot is dot?" while I continued my screeching. Then one of them turned a flashlight in my direction, they saw my head, and everybody laughed.

Our seventy-four men had all the boiled lobster they could eat for breakfast. How tender and sweet those little lobsters were! The shucks or shells were saved for the hens, and they seemed to like them.

Cape Horn winds continued pretty tame in the first two days after we crossed the boundary, but I told the captain and Charlie at dinner that I wasn't going to give up wishing for a real rip-snorter before we got around.

The water we were sailing through next day looked as black as ink, although perfectly clear and clean. Rain squalls hovered around, and there was much pulling and hauling, and taking in and setting of sails because of the changeable winds. One riotous squall caught us with every stitch of canvas set. Six men heaved at the steering wheel to luff her before she should go over bottom side up. Sails and yards came down on the run, but the scud soon passed.

In one calm spell the waves made a great slapping and plopping noise by jumping up two or three feet in points like pyramids. It gave me a queer feeling with other things so quiet, even though I knew perfectly well that it was caused simply by the meeting of opposing currents.

Thursday, about sixty miles east of Staten Island, the captain and mate got together and made a delicate wind-direction indicator of a feather, so they could tell where the wind was coming from. What a queer occupation off Cape Horn, the reputed home of all sorts of violent storms! It was colder now than at any time in the North Sea.

We started eating the Christmas fruit cake, and treasured every crumb.

That morning we had what the captain called "American hash." He said: "I think dot I vill not eat any this time."

Charlie and I asked him, "Why not?"

And he replied, "There is too much of fresh meat in dot hash."

We wondered what he meant. Here we were two months at sea and he was talking about fresh meat, but anyhow we liked it and ate two helpings.

When we finished, the captain said, "Vas dot good?"

Just then the cook came in and asked him to dress his finger again, and we learned that while grinding the hash meat, the end of one finger had been taken off by the grinder. The captain had known this all the time. "You two fellers vas cannibals," he said, and he laughed at us for the next two weeks.

A killer whale, half black and half white, played around the ship for an hour or so Friday. It is a small sort of whale, but the most ferocious of all the tribe, and it kills whales ten times its size.

Charlie and the captain were sore at me because I wished for a rip-snorter storm. But there was no sign yet of anything of that kind.

I finished "The Outline of History" and had learned a lot from it. Another book I read was Dana's "Vacation Voyage to Cuba." It didn't suit me nearly as well as his "Two Years Before the Mast." He seemed to have tried to write a book without having enough to say.

February 8th came with nice cold weather and a moderate breeze, and I couldn't help thinking how awfully disappointed I would be if we got around the Horn without at least a gale. The last two or three years vessels had seen plenty of ice where we were—even as many as a hundred bergs at the same time. I hoped we would go far enough south to get a look at some, but of course it is dangerous sailing anywhere near them.

Sunday, the 9th, the wish that I first made at the Giants Causeway came true. A real storm got started that morning and gathered headway all day. "Mine eyes have seen the glory of the coming of the *wind,*" but what I saw while the storm lasted can't be told in words. The log book showed a number twelve hurricane, long before the worst came. A tremendous sea had worked up that gave a show worth the whole trip. We were hove to and shortened down to the lower tops'ls and two stays'ls.

The blowing spray and flying spume turned the surface of the ocean white, except for faint grayish streaks, and the water around the ship and as far away as I could see had the appearance of being blanketed with snow. Meanwhile the wind was roaring and screeching through the rigging with sounds as if a lot of savage beasts were fighting, threatening, and clawing up there.

I always had wanted to see a big, heavy sail blow away in a hurricane, and now came my chance. The steel wire three quarters of an inch in diameter around the edge of the main lower tops'l broke with a noise that made me think some one had shot off a cannon. The canvas was the very heaviest made, and brand new, so it didn't all go at once, but banged and snapped making a racket like a machine gun. If anyone had told me canvas could make such a noise I would have said, "Tell that to the marines."

When the wire broke and the sail began to go, I was on deck. "Here's a great chance for moving pictures," I thought. So I got the camera in a hurry and buzzed away at the shredding sail, while a lone sailor went out to the end of the yard to let go the preventer sheet. If that banging sail had hit him once, it would have killed him. But he succeeded in letting go the sheet. Then a score of other sailors climbed up and joined him, and they furled what was left of the sail.

The third mate was on the leeward end of the yard where a narrow strip of canvas streamed out beyond reach. He had been taught to save every scrap of material, and he let himself hang down from a heavy wire by one hand and a leg, while he reached for the fragment of sail.

The captain down below yelled and blew his whistle as loud as he could trying to stop him, but even those on deck within ten feet of the captain could hardly hear his voice above the screeching and howling of the storm.

So the strip of canvas was saved.

At times water blew along the surface of the sea like a fog, and the wind was so fierce it couldn't be faced. While the captain and I were eating dinner there was a jarring crash that felt and sounded like hitting a rock. The captain jumped up exclaiming, "Mine Gott! Ist der mast gone?"

On deck we found that a terrific wave had struck the port side of the ship, and the captain ordered the carpenter to sound the wells to see if she were leaking. In ten or fifteen minutes the carpenter returned and reported, "No water in the wells."

However, further inspection revealed that a whole section of the side of the ship, twenty feet across, was bent in, steel plates, frames, and all. Yet the only places that water was coming through the sides was where the sea had broken the glass in some portholes. The skipper said he never had heard of a wave bending in the side of such a ship before.

I thought I would go up to the main royal yard to see if I could hold on under such conditions.

After waiting until the captain went below, so he wouldn't stop me, I started. But just then the second mate, who had charge of the watch, called out, "You can't go up there!"

"I have to go," I told him. "This is what I've come to Cape Horn for."

"No," he insisted. "You'll get blown off or shaken off."

I didn't agree with him, and he finally said, "Well, you go on your own responsibility. I'm not to blame, whatever happens to you."

"All right," I said and went on up.

When I had gone about to the height of the upper top'sl yard, a sea smashed against the windward side of the ship and sent spray over my head. It takes some force to shoot water up that high against such a gale. Meanwhile the sun occasionally shone down on all the confusion and violence and made dainty rainbows in the flying scud.

As I neared the top of the mast I would stop whenever the ship rolled to windward, because I had such difficulty in pulling my feet back

Off Cape Horn

Cranking the fog horn

Catting the anchors

against the wind and getting them up to the next ratline. The air rushed past me at about one hundred and fifty miles an hour, making a horrible screeching howl such as I never had heard before.

The top of the mast swung in an arc fully three hundred feet at some of the rolls, and these rolls of forty-five degrees often were made in eleven seconds.

On at least twenty of the ship's rolls to windward I tried the experiment of hollering just as loud as I could. Yet it was impossible to hear myself. Not the least whisper reached me of the loud noise I must have made. I wouldn't have thought that possible. Once I tried to holler to windward, but nearly a barrelful of the hurricane was driven down my throat, and I gave up that sort of experimenting.

It was necessary to be very careful of my lips and hold them tight or the wind would take charge of them. Yet they had to be parted enough to let in some air, as one's nose is useless for breathing purposes in a hurricane.

A light shower caught me at the top of the

mast, and some scattered drops that struck the back of my neck felt like so many birdshot.

I had demonstrated to myself that it was possible to hold on, and I went down, got my movie camera, and returned to the mast-top. After tangling my arms and legs up in the ratlines to keep from blowing away, I took movies of the Cape Horn gray backs that went sweeping across the deck of the ship a hundred and seventy-five feet below me. That downlook onto the churning sea as it battered the old *Peking* and kept filling her decks with its writhing waters, was the grandest sight I ever had looked on.

The water got into the ship everywhere, except the cargo hold, and a dozen boys were kept busy bailing out. Most of the sailors slept on the spare sails in the sail locker because their foc'sle was so filled with water. Such big seas came aboard that they couldn't open the foc'sle door, and the only way they could enter was by the skylight.

To go into a foc'sle half full of water during such a storm, with sea chests, bunk boards, and suit cases banging and crashing at each roll, was just looking for death. Down below deck the ship creaked as if she might break up at any minute.

In the night the steering cable that led to the midships wheel broke. The after wheel was stuck, and the spanker had to be set to keep the vessel up into the wind until the cable was fixed.

At noon on Monday we had been driven back eighty-four miles since the previous noon. We took down what was left of the lower tops'l that blew out and set another in its place.

I got a piece of the torn sail and started to make a sea bag of it. That was something I would need if we ever got to port. Nearly every sailing-ship seaman has a sea bag. He keeps his clothes in it, and usually has made it himself.

One thing we lost in the storm was our shark's tail at the tip of the jib boom. "That was our fair weather charm," I said to Charlie, "and it's gone."

"Small loss," was his response. "Mighty little good it's done us on this trip."

"But you can't tell how much worse the weather might have been without it," I suggested.

"Humph!" he growled, "*no* weather could be worse! I know that."

A shark's tail is tough, and ours had been firmly spiked on. Besides, it was fifty feet above the water level, yet some wave must have reached it and given it an awful wallop, or it couldn't have been torn loose.

Monday night we had eight sails set, as there was far less wind and the waves were smaller. Nevertheless there was wind enough to blow out the mizzen topmast stays'l when we tried to set it. All the crew were kept busy repairing the damage done by the storm. There was a snow-squall in the afternoon, and when it was over we had a snowball fight. Cape Horn snow doesn't fall in flakes, but in little pellets like hail. It is known as Cape Horn sugar. The thermometer registered a little above freezing, which is as cold as the dickens at sea.

We saw Cape Horn Tuesday morning. It rises abruptly to a height of fourteen hundred feet so it can be seen forty miles on a clear day. We were lucky to see it at all, for most ships go around the Horn without getting a sight of land. This was the first we had seen since passing the Isle of Wight about two months before.

The wind was light and it shifted every hour or so. That kept us hauling sails up and down and bracing yards half the time. When the wind shifted, we took in all sail aft of the mizzen mast and hauled up the mains'l and cro'jack in the buntlines. Each watch that was off duty did what it could to clear up the mess the sea had made of their foc'sle.

There were head winds nearly all the time for several days, so that on Wednesday we were only ten miles from where we had been Sunday noon. The nights were very short and we had gone south so far that it was not really dark even at midnight.

I finished making the sea bag, and I was sure it wouldn't rip. The heavy canvas and double seams would take care of that.

February 13th was Charlie's birthday. He

was twenty-four; so I whaled him twenty-four
times with one extra whale added "to grow on."

The captain celebrated the occasion by order-
ing eggs for our breakfast. The yolks were a deep
blood red, but tasted good if you forgot what
they looked like. Our skipper said the color was
caused by the hen's eating the shells of the little
lobsters. The cooks made a big cake, one and
one-half by two feet, with a fancy 24 on top.
It had a layer of apple in it and tasted fine.

A peach of a storm came up during the night.
It was even better than the one on Sunday! Ac-
cording to the captain, the wind scarcely ever
blows any harder. Summer storms, he claimed,
were shorter, but stronger, than those in winter.
I'd swear to it that some of the waves looped up
to a height well over the fifty feet which it is
said scientific measurements prove to be the
limit. We everlastingly rolled, jumped, wal-
lowed, and dived.

The creakings of the ship under us at such a
time conveyed a sense of suffering—as if she
were in pain and anguish. To hear them after I

had gotten into my bunk, made me feel like
drawing the bedclothes over my head. I wanted
to shut out not only those dismal creakings below deck, but the frightful wailing and snarling
that came to my ears from the rigging.

In general, however, I had a good time getting thrills out of the storms. Every walloping
big wave was a joy—I welcomed it. The wild-
ness of the winds was glorious. There was charm
in all the sights and sounds, and in the ever-vary-
ing motions of the vessel, the waves, and the
clouds. A few weeks more battling in those savage waters at the Horn would have suited me.

But for the crew this was a dreary time of hard-
ship. They were sore and glum, and the glory
of the storms was lost on them. So far as my
feeling was concerned the only time I found a
little dull was between storms.

On two or three occasions, at meal time, the
ship tilted with a lurch that ended in a sharp
jerk and shot those of us who were at the table
out of our chairs. I laughed, but no one else
could see anything funny about it. The skipper

had a pained look on his face and the rest grumbled and cursed.

In that second rip-snorter our barometer went down to 28.19 inches, which is the lowest sea level pressure I ever had seen or that I ever expect to see.

We were told by the captain that there at Cape Horn, a few years earlier, his barometer registered the extremely low pressure of 27.71 inches.

"Wow!" Charlie exclaimed. "And what kind of storms, gales, and hurricanes did you get then, I'd like to know?"

"Ve got not'ing but a flat calm," the skipper answered.

Two years before our trip, the *Peking* made a voyage from Chile to Hamburg in seventy-seven days, and never took in a sail during all that time—an amazing record, and how different from ours!

There was nothing warm for breakfast, and only soup for dinner, but I couldn't blame the cooks. What surprised me was that they were

able to make the soup. Salt water was everywhere inside of the ship's living quarters. I
stayed out on deck in the cold hour after hour
just to watch the waves. No two were alike, and
I always was wondering what the next one would
do. It was while there that I saw the maintop-
mast stays'l leave us for parts unknown; and
every half hour or so a big sea came aboard.
Then, whatever else we did, our chief job was
holding on.

Some months later we learned that when the
Peking was going back round the Horn, one of
these big waves washed five men overboard, leaving that many empty bunks.

It was calm for a while on the morning of the
15th, but the swell from the previous day's storm
hadn't smoothed out and we rolled in fine style.
The only time we were warm in the Cape Horn
vicinity was when we were in bed, or after the
exertion of taking in or setting a sail.

The worst pain I ever remember experien-
cing, was when we were sent aloft to furl
a heavy sail after we had stood on deck several

hours and our hands were thoroughly numb with cold. Even then they seemed to be nearly as strong as when warm, if we gripped something large. After furling sail for a while they limbered up, and we could twink our fingers around like lightning. That was great fun.

Another time that cold hands were a serious discomfort was when we were eating, and tried to cut up "salt horse" with a small knife. We couldn't hold the knife.

One day the barometer went down an inch and two-tenths in seven hours; but then it stopped dead and we got only a moderate gale.

The captain had two boxes of flowers under the skylight that was over the dining-room table. Each box was about four feet long, zinc-lined, and painted green. The captain himself watered and took care of the flowers. Of course they could not thrive in the cold, stormy North Sea weather, but on our way down through the Atlantic the heat and sunshine encouraged them to unfurl their greenery and put forth some scattering blossoms. While we were rounding the Horn the skylights were shut, and the plants got no light to speak of. Worse still, they were drenched with salt water. Now we were in gentler surroundings and the skipper opened the skylights. I happened to be standing close by at the time, and he turned to me exclaiming: "Mine gracious! Look at dot. Der flowers are all dead!"

Yes, and they were a melancholly sight. I was sorry for him.

The next day the barometer went down an inch and two tenths in seven hours; but then it stopped dead so we got only a moderate gale.

Our sailmaker and our blacksmith had a serious argument one day about the latest styles in men's clothes, and they hotly debated the proper color for shoes, socks, neckties, and handkerchiefs. You would have thought they were gentlemen's outfitters in Berlin.

Charlie and I liked to look at the map of New England and read over the names of places we used to know. You have to be away from home a long time to understand what it means to you.

After rounding the Horn and coming safely through the storms, we were interested in looking at the chart which showed our zigzag course when we were trying to beat against the westerly gales.

Once, while we were thus engaged, Charlie suddenly remarked: "See here; the whole southern tip of the continent curves off to the eastward. I think those persistent westerly gales and hurricanes must have something to do with that twist of the coast line."

"That wouldn't surprise me a bit," I said. "Judging from our experience, those storms are equal to anything, even moving mountains."

"Well, then," Charlie went on, "they seem to have torn into the west coast for hundreds of miles north, leaving it ragged with islands and bays while the east coast is left smooth."

And I said: "Notice Tierra del Fuego. That appears to be broken away from the mainland and shoved eastward. Then there's the Falkland Islands. They look as if the gales had torn them to pieces and blown them away out there in the

Atlantic more than three hundred miles from the coast."

The crew had spent most of their time for the last two weeks at the slow, primitive tasks of braiding sennit and plaiting rope yarns.

Monday the 20th we were one hundred and thirty-five miles from shore with a wind that would allow us to sail parallel with the almost straight north and south line of the coast of Chile. But the captain figured that we didn't have enough sea room. So he headed sou'sou'-west back toward the latitudes of Cape Horn.

Charlie found this particularly disturbing. Cape Horn had gotten on his nerves. On the other hand, I was enjoying the experience, and I said to him: "I'm not exactly praying for any more storms as bad as those we've gone through— they're too wearing and troublesome to the crew —but if one could be staged that was a *little* worse I'd like to see what the ship and crew would do in it."

"Oh, raspberries!" he exclaimed. "You've had storms enough on this trip to last a lifetime. I want to get out of here as soon as we can, and we'll never arrive in Chile by heading for the Antarctic."

He was in a more cheerful mood the next morning when the ship turned northerly on her course again, but light head winds prevented our making much progress.

Now fog shut down on us, and although there was no likelihood that any ship was within a thousand miles, our old fashioned foghorn had to be gotten into action. It was a portable chest with a copper funnel, and looked like a gramaphone of the '90s. One of the crew, usually the dumbest man on board, because he was the one who could best be spared from other work, brought it up on the foc'sle, set it on the rail, and by turning a crank, kept it emitting a series of dismal, prolonged hoots. These could hardly have been heard more than the length of the ship, but in case of collision they satisfied the law.

Since leaving Hamburg, Mauritz, the captain's dog, had taken a piece out of all but one of the officers and half the crew. The second mate, who teased him most, had escaped until now, when he got two holes through each of three fingers. The captain thought this was a great joke and spoke kindly to the *dog*. No one could tell at any particular time whether Mauritz was playing or angry.

One of the boys with a bad boil came to the captain's cabin for treatment, and the captain, as a part of his curative efforts, cut down to the bone and then squeezed the boil so hard that a sudden spurt of pus and blood flew fifteen feet up in the sky-light. He sometimes used all the strength of his great arms and hands in the boil-pinching.

On Thursday, February 20th, the last of our fruit cake was eaten. We thought it was the best thing we could have had in the food line for a trip such as this. And there was a sentiment about it that added to its flavor.

The next day we completed the rounding of Cape Horn—a nineteen days' voyage. Rather slow, but ships have been known to take two months. On the other hand, favoring winds make possible a minimum of a week. This was our first day of real sunshine for a long time.

The captain put the dog in the pen with the pigs, but they were so fat he couldn't bite them except when he got hold of their tails. Then what a noise they did make!

Saturday the sky was overcast all day, and there were queer cloud formations at the horizon that looked like forest fires with the gray smoke blowing off to one side. I finished making a blue silk, square-knot necktie for myself.

On the morrow a north wind made our course a dead beat to windward, so we only made forty-four miles in twenty-four hours. A school of eight or ten fair-sized whales came spouting and blowing along beside the vessel. Then they disappeared, and a minute later we saw them on the other side. They must have swum right under the ship.

Monday we had a fair wind at last and went plowing along in good shape. The captain caught some of the crew in the foc'sle when it was their watch on deck. They were so scared, that in their haste to get out they piled up on top of each other filling the whole doorway.

Our noon sights the next day showed that only four hundred and fifty miles lay between us and port. The ship, with the whole crew shining brass or painting, was beginning to look like a yacht. This was a sure sign that we were nearing our destination.

The captain told Charlie and me about a sure cure for a cancer that is near the outside of the body. The cancer must be cut into a little, and a live frog bound against the cut. When the frog dies it should be replaced by a live one, and so on until the cure was complete. A friend of the captain's was cured that way.

On Wednesday we were ninety days out, and we wondered what had happened in the world since we left it. We had been free from all troubles except our own.

The skipper lent me a sea adventure book in which I read about a fellow who came down the edge of sails from one yard to another; so I had to find out whether I could do that. I never realized before the satisfaction there is in having your fingers around something dependable when you are up aloft in the rigging. You can't get a grip that gives you any confidence while clinging to the edge of a sail.

I came down the edge of the upper and lower tops'ls, hand under hand, and it was a ticklish thing to do because there was almost nothing to grip on. I could only pinch the edge of the canvas with one hand after the other, and always fingers and thumbs had to be held perfectly straight while making that awkward pinch on the canvas. Another thing I did was to go down the fore-royal headstay from the top of the mast to the end of the jib boom, a distance of one hundred and seventy-five feet. Charlie took moving pictures of both these stunts.

One huge, lone sea jumped aboard without warning that morning. It caught several fellows napping and properly soaked them.

During the day the anchor chains were shackled on, and the anchors catted over the bow ready to let go. Charlie and I washed all our clothes and were prepared to leave promptly when the time came.

Friday the captain began to talk about the prospect of sighting land soon. So just after figuring out our noon position, I went up to the main royal taking along the skipper's binoculars. From there I scanned the eastern horizon. It was a fine, clear day, and sure enough there was the land, although not much more than a blur. I shouted down, "Land O, two points forward of the starboard beam!"

This was a big event, and shore clothes began to be hung out to air. They certainly needed it. Some were so mouldy you would think they were made of white fur rather than of real cloth. They didn't look as if they ever would be fit to wear again. In the evening the mates were full of life, taking cross-bearings of lighthouses, and Charlie and I packed our sea bags in accord with the custom of all real sailors before reaching port.

Saturday morning, March 1st, we were just outside of Talcahuano harbor, about three hundred miles south of Valparaiso. Charlie was the most pleased of any of us to find himself close to land once more. And he said, smiling in delight as he looked toward shore, "Isn't that a marvelous sight!"

I couldn't see anything particularly attractive about it; but Charlie was in an ecstasy. He even forgave the captain's dog, against which he had treasured a grudge ever since being bitten by the beast. But now he said, "Mauritz, you're a good old dog after all."

A little tug came to take our towline, but instead, the captain arranged to have her take me for a little trip circling around to get moving pictures of the *Peking* under full sail. I climbed up on our ship's rail and went down a line hand over hand to the deck of the tug with my movie camera over my shoulder. When I finished taking the pictures we returned along side of the *Peking,* and I climbed back on deck. Then we took the towline, and with the almost negligible help of the tug, which had a big smokestack

Talcahuano's most powerful tug

Unloading coke into a lighter

A fruit seller comes aboard

"The old man" going ashore
in the captain's gig

and a loud whistle, but no power, we beat our way up to the anchorage.

There we made lively work of taking in sail while rounding up to drop our anchor about a mile from the town.

Charlie and I hadn't a cent to our names, but we borrowed some money from the captain. Then, each with a sea bag and suitcase, and Charlie with a knapsack besides, we went down the gangway and stepped into the harbor master's little motor boat which was to take us to the town.

The crew left work, climbed up on the rail, and as the boat shoved off waved their hats and gave us three rousing cheers. Then we stood up in the boat waving and cheering in response, and feeling a keen regret that we were parting from our friendly shipmates and leaving behind the stately *Peking,* which had been our home on the ninety-three days' voyage from Hamburg in Germany to the South American port of Talcahuano in Chile.

The *Peking* with the crew gathered on the poop deck

AFTERWORD

FORTY-EIGHT YEARS LATER

In 1977 we asked Captain Johnson to write about the voyage in light of his later experience at sea. Reluctant at first, he responded to our urgings and turned out this classic essay on what it took to sail a ship like the Peking.

Looking back forty-eight years I now write this chapter from the vantage point of experience, changing values and many years as a captain, seldom allowed an author-sailor. The fact that *Peking* is still alive today, beautifully preserved and on display at South Street Seaport Museum in New York City gives me a more vital basis from which to reminisce about my Cape Horn voyage.

Luckily my father, who was a writer, taught me to jot down items of interest as they occurred daily. As I reread the book, I am astonished that so many forgotten details are spelled out just as they happened. At the same time a few mistakes are detected, such as two cases where I use the term "knots per hour" instead of simply "knots." A knot means nautical miles per hour.

Other than seeing these small errors I find I want

157

to add some memories of things that were too close for me to see significantly at the time. For one thing it now needs explaining that rounding the Horn is a longer job than anyone concludes from a map. We knew that we weren't around until we had sailed 200 miles west and then north to Latitude 50 South, and not just past that notorious point of land. Every Laeisz ship was required, with no exceptions, to beat out to the west that far before turning north.

I have found this fact is not generally known, but it is one of the reasons why Cape Horn is such an ordeal when westward bound. Since making the voyage I have heard of several captains cutting this corner and either losing their ships or being driven back amongst the islands and rocks with the vessel practically out of control. After a few weeks of battling the Horn there is a great urge to get out of this foul weather, but Captain Jurs, like the magnificent seaman he was, beat against the westerlies to the last mile.

As a contrast to the normal weather at Cape Horn I actually landed on Horn Island in January 1977 during a beautiful smooth spell. Sailing vessels always stayed away from Cape Stiff in case a shift of wind should blow them onto this cruel shore. This visit brought back memories of the long drawn out battles many ships had off this cape. Hundreds of them, including HMS *Bounty,* and especially in 1905, a year of particularly infamous storms, gave up the struggle and sailed the other way around the world to their destinations. Many lost their rigs overboard and put in to Port Stanley in the Falkland Islands for repairs or for sale as hulks in which to store wool. Others just plain went down in the attempt and were never heard of again. All these stories, of which I have read so many, have a far deeper meaning if one has struggled aboard a huge square rigger driven backwards and forwards by the gales while the palms of your hands disintegrate in your fight with the sails in snow storms.

I have also noted through the years that many vessels make good passages around the Horn in both directions, but what is there to read about if you have a smooth sea? So naturally most of these roundings go unnoticed. I am therefore forever thankful that my one Cape Horn passage was through storms that even the skipper, a veteran of fifty-odd roundings, said were among the most severe he had ever encountered.

As a boy back on the farm in Massachusetts' Connecticut Valley I was the State 4-H Club corn raising champion for two years. (I know now that old time skippers believed that, if they could not get a seaman, they would choose a farm boy.) Many years of agricultural courses at school supposedly prepared me for the life of a farmer.

But aside from those courses I was reading with more enthusiasm of bold adventure, particularly in sailing ships with emphasis on Cape Horn. I carefully noted the disadvantages of poor food and even a soaking bunk, the extreme cold and all the dangers of being flung from a yard or being smashed on deck by a monster sea. I couldn't change those prospects, but a big feature of Jack London's books particularly was the fighting that went on aboard ship. I figured I could do something about that, so I secretly sent off for a physical culture course and carried out the instructions religiously. Further books on wrestling, jiu jitsu and acrobatics followed. I trained till I could stand on my head on top of every telephone pole within a half mile of home. The result was that, being prepared ahead of time, I never had a fight. But physical strength, even unused in combat, was well worth my training for shipmates, and even a skipper, appreciate a man who can pull, jerk, heave, lift and climb in a way that counts.

Some of the books had mentioned young men climbing aloft on their first experience and freezing clamped to the rigging unable to work on the sails till further tries accustomed them to the height and vibrations of the rig. Here is where my telephone pole training stood me in good stead when furling sail seventeen stories above the deck. By the time we were off Cape Horn I was able to chin myself with one finger.

A final benefit of all my training was in taking movies from the top of the mast with winds in the vicinity of 100 miles per hour. These very pictures I showed to the Honourable Company of Master Mariners in London in 1930. Every man in the audience was a square-rigger skipper or retired and they collectively must have represented several thousand times around Cape Horn. After the show they came up and said not a man in the audience had seen that much water across the deck of a ship unless she was sunk. They also said they knew such pictures had never been taken and what's more never would be taken and therefore asked to chip in right then to get a copy for the British Museum. I was able to supply the pictures and felt proud of pleasing these old timers. I realized that their ships were smaller than the big Flying P barks and many were built of wood rather than steel. Such ships didn't take such a weight of water on deck and would not have survived it if they had.

At the time I had no idea of the importance of what they wanted as I had made only one Cape Horn voyage and thought others must have taken better pictures than I on some occasion. However, the chance never occurred as the very early days of 16mm movie film coincided with the demise of the cargo-carrying square riggers westward bound, loaded to their marks, and acting like halftide rocks.

From my first boarding of the *Peking* to the end of the voyage I found an incredible use of human hands

was taken for granted. All the power to move anything and cause anything to happen to force that
8,000 tons of ship and cargo to make this voyage
came through human hands. There were no motors,
no valves, no switches, no lights for working about
the deck of aloft, only hands, hands, and more
hands, gripping, working, struggling to prolong
your life and force that mammoth ship against her
will to carry that cargo to Chile. In the tropics or in
reasonable weather this was all very well, but in the
vicinity of Cape Horn, where it snows every month
of the year, our hands took on the appearance of
rough claws with cracks through the heavy skin
parallel with our fingers and deep enough to allow a
bit of blood to ooze through on every gripping of the
shrouds or sails. In the ships of the Flying P Line no
one ever wore gloves. I had some, but wouldn't have
been caught dead wearing them as no one else did.

We had never heard of chill factor in those days,
but with your hands wet, numb with the cold, hanging out of oilskins with a few boils or chafed places
around your wrists, they were in continuous pain especially when we were ordered aloft to furl sail.

When exercise brought life back into them, I found the pain excruciating. I remember saying thousands of times that in order to appreciate the Cape Horn battle, one must be able to forget about his hands and wrists completely.

In the same way it was also taken for granted that you could sleep in soaking clothes as there was no other way to dry them out. I had two pairs of heavy underwear, but used only one as there was no use changing them and getting the other pair wet without a place to dry anything. It is fairly obvious that only a diver's suit would keep you dry where thousands of tons of water swept the deck submerging the crew time and again. Incidentally it was very dangerous to be in a position where you have to swim on the deck as the Second Mate did when he got caught in the wrong place at the wrong second.

It is only in the years since this book was written that I have time to appreciate one thing that was going on before my eyes. In the sailing of a big ship in foul weather there is a remarkable force of some kind that makes scores of ordinary men surpass themselves in feats of strength, effectiveness and daring. I was astonished to observe time and again the almost complete disregard of self when the ship badly needed something done. Men would go out along the yards on those dangling footropes with the ship rolling topgallant bulwarks under. They would claw for a whipping piece of canvas that could knock them galley west. They would scramble out onto the bowsprit though it was diving out of sight and a mean sea could tear them off. Danger threatened alow and aloft, but when the ship needed them, these young seamen got on with the job regardless.

Many a sailor turns into a hero with none of the blare of publicity and crowds that hail the star on the athletic field. I believe he is in a sort of trance or perhaps hypnotized by the extreme need of the ship. That is why steamship companies subsidize the training of these boys under sail. Later they may be officers aboard a steamer, but they will have learned to do for the ship as they never would under power. You might call it the religion of sail.

The loveliest part of the voyage and satisfying to me in every way was everything to do with the sails. Under the direction of the sailmaker I not only repaired sails, but made brand new ones. This knowledge was most useful in my later years of sailing around the world. All the work was done by hand with no sewing machine. The canvas was extremely heavy double aught hemp requiring strong fingers to sew a good seam.

Now again when hands had made the sails, bent them on the yards aloft, set and furled them when wind dictated and the captain ordered. Hands hauled on sheets adjusting the angle of the sails innumerable times with changing winds and courses. Then through our hands sails made contact with the unseen wind to move this great ship. Here I was close to the secret of why we go to sea. There is an indefinable knowledge, an art, in getting the best out of wind and sails, fascinating to me in the complexity of a 4-mast bark with her great fabric of lines, rigging, spars and canvas—and available crew.

After these many years of voyaging as captain of my own ships around the world I have even greater appreciation for Captain Jurs's ability as the complete seaman. That included such accomplishments as setting arms and legs of battered sailors. This brings to mind his story about a previous trip when he set a seaman's broken leg, splinting it securely. That night the sailor felt the splints were causing him unbearable pain, so he removed them. The captain said it took all his strength to pull the tightened muscles enough to get the bones in line again. Then with what fierceness he would have put on the new splints. He concluded, ''I lashed him in his bunk until he couldn't move a millimeter and that leg came out straight, I can tell you. I never set one that didn't!''

Another story was told by the mates of the captain's extraordinary prowess during a storm on a previous voyage. They recounted with considerable awe his seeing a man washed overboard forward. He ran aft, grabbed the spanker sheet with one hand, jumped over the stern into the boiling maelstrom, seized the sailor's hair with the other hand and was pulled back aboard with that one tremendous grip sufficing for two. This they claim was done not once, but twice. Neither they nor I have ever seen it written up, nor mentioned in any of the literature of Cape Horn, but my hat's off to Captain Jurs in more ways than one.

I once asked him if he had ever trained as a wrestler or boxer. "No," he said.

"Did you ever get in a fight?"

"Yes. I hit him first," was all he said

Captain Jurs never had disciplinary troubles. At one time he was Chief Mate of the *Preussen,* known as one of the best all-round seamen as well as possibly the most powerful man afloat in the Flying P Line. Even though he was now middle-aged his physical strength left no doubt that he would be the last fellow on board anyone would want to tangle with. He therefore had no need to stand on his dignity, but would give a hand hauling on lines with the crew or talk freely with any man aboard. We all knew he could do a better job than we could at anything on the ship. He had a temper that frightened the crew in many cases, but it had the advantage of keeping them on their toes to a remarkable degree. You would see the young fellows come on watch and immediately go to the pin rails or fife rails checking over every single line in their part of the ship just in case the previous watch had been the least bit slipshod. It was this standard he set, though often in a somewhat harsh way, that kept the ship sailing smartly and safely, insurance to the life of the men and the delivery of the cargo.

I am sure that my surviving over these many years as seaman and skipper was due in large measure to watching Captain Jurs in action. Luckily I was just old enough with just enough experience behind me to realize that here was a ready-made opportunity to observe what it takes to make fifty-some Cape Horn voyages successfully. As I went on to my own ships I aimed to do things as he would have done them. With him it was never a case of "good enough." There was only his way and I could see that it was practically always the right way. Many decisions I took on the afterdeck in later years were unconsciously dictated by that master. When I succeeded, I would have had his approval. There was always a bit of him on the *Yankee,* and it was a saving bit. He could never have imagined the contribution he was making to young Americans world cruising in my schooner and brigantine. He must have made the difference to other men who served under him as long as they remained in sail. I never saw him again after I left *Peking.* I believe he made only one more round trip in her.

As for the rest of my shipmates, Charlie and I have kept in touch through his career of teaching history in boys' schools and finally at the American University in Beirut. Now retired, he lives not far away in Vermont so we see each other a couple of times a year. Of the German boys I have seen only a few. Some were undoubtedly killed in the war. One Hamburg businessman called on *Yankee* when our ketch was in that port. Another wrote asking for a few pictures as his were lost during the war. I hear of *Peking* sailors older than I showing up at South Street Seaport to lay eyes once more on their old Cape Horner. Shipmates go their various ways and don't often meet again, but when they do, what memories!

It is now an enormous satisfaction to me that *Peking* has survived the years when most other square riggers of her sort have disappeared from the seas. It is especially gratifying to see her at South Street Seaport ready and able to educate the millions who will cross her decks as to how men's hands can cause sails to harness the available winds to push 8,000 tons of her and her cargo the wrong way around the Horn. It is expected that some of my storm movies will be shown aboard to visitors as they pass through the ship and this book will be available to those who want to delve deeper into the hundreds of little happenings that go to make up the delivery of cargo.

Rereading my youthful account of *Peking* forcibly brings to mind the vast change in attitudes toward equipment. The mates watched to save every little piece of string or bit of canvas. We were trained not to waste or break things because no one could order up replacements. It was best to prevent damage, but, once it occurred we then had to make it good by our own efforts. There was no telephone call for a repair man and port was months away. What a contrast to the casual way we now expand and dispose of material. But this self-reliance is still needed at times and where can it be learned now as we did on *Peking?*

I longed to possess Captain Jurs's knowledge of ships and the sea. I met another square-rigger skipper who, after losing his masts, had fixed up a jury rig at sea and brought his vessel into port two months late, but cargo intact. I explained to him how I was waiting for the day when I would know what to do in a case like that.

His remarkable answer was, "Look here, young fellow, something different always happens each time, so you never know what to do, but, listen to me, you've got to bloody well do *something*!" I was able to use that advice the next forty-seven years.

The Flying P Line vessels are regarded as the culmination of efficient delivery of cargo under square rig. Our ideas of human safely have changed drastically since I sailed in her. The thought of one hand for yourself and one for the ship was truly impossible there. I defy anyone to furl those sails with one hand. You furled them with both hands and hung on with your stomach. Nowadays they use lifelines and harnesses such as we never heard of. I well remember the first yachts that showed up with handrails around the deck. I called them fences for sheep or goats. Now practically every yacht in the world, including mine, has them. In contrast to the old days, there being no more loaded square riggers, men are reaching out to new challenges. They organize themselves into racing crews and race around the world, sometimes with greater loss of life percentage wise than square riggers had. Conditions on some of these racers, except perhaps for the food, are just as desperate because of racing as we ever found aboard *Peking.* Of course the *Peking* herself was racing against time and the skipper drove her for all she was worth. But her reason for being was only one thing: carry cargo. There was no slightest use for her being there at all unless the cargo was delivered to the port of destination in good shape. "Cargo is king." We fought with our lives to deliver it just as the racing men fight for their lives for the honor of beating other vessels into port.

Now we go to sea with not only electric lights, power winches, auxiliary motors and sewing machines, but even with radio, loran, echo sounders backed up by computers and satellites. We have changed the terms of the challenge at sea, but we have not changed the sea itself nor ordered the weather. The sea is still a place to learn and train and overcome. But I am glad that my education was aboard the *Peking* where the call for ''all hands'' had its literal meaning.

IRVING JOHNSON

CHARLIE'S VIEW

Charles Brodhead, the ubiquitous, good-natured "Charlie" whom Irving quotes so often in his narrative, joined Irving on the *Peking*'s voyage as what he calls "a last fling" before marrying his college sweetheart Susan Bassett and taking up the distinguished career he went on to establish as history teacher and assistant headmaster in boys' schools. He had graduated from Princeton in the spring of 1929 and decided, as so many have before him, to see some more of the world before settling down—though surely few would do what he did in joining with another young man he'd never met before to cross the ocean and sign on aboard a working windship in the tough Cape Horn trade!

On summer vacations from Princeton he had served in the Standard Oil tanker *Walter Jennings*, and going to New York to roam the waterfront for another seagoing berth after graduation, he landed a job as ordinary seaman aboard the giant liner *Leviathan*, the former German *Vaterland*, masterpiece of Albert Ballin and the biggest ocean liner in the world.

One round trip seemed to have slaked his interest in serving in an ocean liner and he signed on a cargo ship leaving New York for Boston, where she was to pick up cargo for Europe. In Boston, however, he received a telegram from his brother urging him to join Irving Johnson in the *Peking* venture. And the rest, as they say, is history.

To Charlie, as he explained to us at age ninety in his

175

home in the forested hills of southern Vermont, the voyage was to be a literary adventure. He had a copy of the *Oxford Book of English Verse* with him, and sixty-six years after the voyage, he delighted in comparing its various phases to Coleridge's "Rime of the Ancient Mariner." In the Doldrums, they were indeed as still as "a painted ship upon a painted ocean," and while they never encountered the "mast-high" ice, "as green as emerald," which the Ancient Mariner encountered, they did keep blowing a foghorn off Cape Horn to catch an echo off any nearby ice before they ran into it.

Another book he had brought with him was H.G. Wells's *Outline of History.* Irving, always on the look-out for new worlds to explore, soon took over this lengthy tome for his own reading. He also carefully wrote up his journal every day, and Charlie says he was all over the ship studying every part of the great wind-harnessing rig and how things were done aboard—occasionally, he suggests to the annoyance of the hard-working mates and irascible Captain Jurs. In talking of their first weeks at sea, Charlie cleared up a small mystery for us. How did Irving manage to be always at the scene of action, when big things like an anchor breaking loose were going on?

The answer is that as paying passengers, Irving and Charlie did not stand regular watches or have assigned duties. They paid a small fee of $1 per day, but the connections Irving had through his boss Carlton

Newcomb of Western Union—owner of the yacht *Charmian* in which Irving served as professional skipper—were enough for the two young men to be accorded special treatment. They dined with Captain Jurs, as Irving's narrative makes clear, not with the crew. We may be grateful for this arrangement, since it made possible much of the extraordinary detail and accuracy of Irving's book. As Charlie puts it, Newcomb had literally and figuratively "pulled wires" to get them aboard the ship. The underlying attitude of the German owners is revealed in Irving's account of the earnest talk they were given in an evident attempt to dissuade them from going, at the risk of life and limb and possible high-level corporate repercussions.

In answer to the question "Did you ever wonder why on earth you'd signed on for this tough trip?" Charlie immediately responded: "Yes! Quite often." When the ship was embayed behind the Hook of Holland in hurricane winds, Charlie remembers Captain Jurs telling the two young men that the vessel was probably doomed to be driven ashore. What happens then? "Den, boys, I guess we lose the ship." Charlie strapped his journal to his waist, after making a final (it seemed then) entry: "If we don't get out of this, good-bye, Susan." But Charlie's doubts seem to have worn away as the various emergencies of the voyage were met and overcome, and Charlie says Irving never faltered—he reveled in the heavy weather and was always up and about observing and sharing the work of the ship.

Once out in the broad Atlantic, Charlie asked to stand regular watches. He had a lot to learn, some of it painful, as when the order was given to loose the sheet of one of the staysails while tacking ship. Charlie jumped to cast off the sheet and found himself lifted off the deck and dumped back repeatedly until a watchmate came to his rescue. "I hadn't realized this was always a two-man job," he observed with a grin.

The German cadets aboard were paid 28 cents a day for the privilege of working the ship under the direction of the small professional crew. They were driven and driven hard, as Irving's narrative makes clear. Did Charlie think they were too badly treated? No, not really. It was a rough life. The only example of physical punishment he could remember occurred when one "rather supercilious" cadet whose father was a German shipping magnate, failed to properly turn in a splice in a wire. The whole watch was learning together, and evidently Captain Jurs decided this inattentive student needed to be taken down a peg. Jurs roared at him and beat him on the chest with a rope's end. It was probably painful and intimidating, but no real harm was done. One gets the impression that Charlie felt this treatment was good for the obstreperous 16-year-old, who was in Charlie's watch.

The language spoken aboard ship was Low German, the language of the Frisian Islands fringing Germany's

North Sea coast. This medieval language is much closer to English than is High German, the standard language of the German nation. From an early date, the young Americans had little trouble in understanding what was said about the decks. With his literary interests, Charlie was fascinated by the rituals observed aboard. He was particularly moved by the change-of-watch order "Change helmsman and lookout"—the order being given by the mate in slow cadence and precisely repeated back by the full watch in a slow, united chant. Charlie remembered this vividly across the span of nearly seven decades as an expression of that solemn dedication to the ship which underlay all the rough business of life aboard.

*   *   *   *   *

When Charlie arrived back in New York with Irving in May 1930, he had money left over from the sum he'd set aside for the *Peking* adventure, so he spent it on a rough-and-ready tour of the USSR. Returning from that wild excursion, traveling 3rd class over the Russian railways, he embarked for home on a liner that overtook the *Peking* standing down the English Channel on her last run as a commercial sailing ship, under Captain Jurs's command. One can imagine his feelings as he looked across at the ship that had been his home, his place of learning and of the beginning of his life-long friendship with Captain Irving Johnson.

Two years later, in 1932, he married Susan Bassett,

and after a honeymoon in Norway, in which the adventurous couple hiked the glaciers, they went to the German seaport city of Hamburg. There they found that the *Peking* had been sold as a training ship, renamed *Arethusa*, and was moored in the Medway in England, near the mouth of the Thames River. Captain Jurs had retired to a cottage downstream on the Elbe.

Captain Jurs came up to Hamburg to see the film that Irving Johnson had made with Charlie's help. Jurs was horrified when he saw Johnson coming down the leach of a squaresail hand over hand. "That fellow Yonson," Charlie remembers him saying, "if I could get my hands on him, I wring his neck!" Things got worse when he saw Irving waving his hands perched on a yard-arm and then sliding down the fore royal stay. No doubt the dreaded "repercussions" were running through the Captain's mind. But then, it is apparent that Jurs was not one to hold his feelings about things in check!

Charlie signed off from the voyage with a certification of his service as Ordinary Seaman (OS), Irving with a certification as Able-Bodied Seaman (AB).

* * * * *

After our visit with Charlie, Norma Stanford and I rolled on down the highway to the Johnson farm on the banks of the Connecticut River in South Hadley, Massachusetts. Exy had lunch waiting for us and we found ourselves talking around the table about historic ship preservation and sail training. Exy observed that three ships closely linked to Irving's life had been preserved. In addition to the *Peking*, the schooner *Wander Bird*, aboard which Exy and Irving first met, has been lovingly restored to sailing condition by Harold Sommer in San Francisco. Irving and Exy sailed her in a strong breeze on the Bay in 1986. And the elegant J-boat *Shamrock V*, in which Irving had sailed to England after the *Peking* voyage, has been brought back to her 1930s splendor by Elizabeth Meyer of the International Yacht Restoration School in Newport, Rhode Island.

The steel brigantine *Yankee* was lost on a Pacific atoll after the Johnsons sold her, but her near sisters, the schooner *Westward* and brigantine *Corwith Cramer*, are actively campaigned out of Woods Hole, Cape Cod,

Exy uses a light touch at the helm of the SEA schooner *Westward* in January 1995, with Captain Sean Bercaw. Sean is the son of Jay Bercaw, chief mate on the Johnsons' fifth and sixth circumnavigations in the brigantine *Yankee*.

by the Sea Education Association. Exy, who went to sea twice in 1995 in the SEA program, considers it the finest sailing educational experience offered today. And she should know, for she keeps up with every aspect of the game, from chantey singing to traditional navigation, which is still practiced aboard these handsome, completely seaworthy vessels.

Irving played an important role as Trustee of SEA, and it is good to know also that the *Peking* is home base for multifarious educational programs in her berth at the South Street Seaport Museum. For the more casual visitor, Irving's film of the Cape Horn voyage of 1929-30 is shown continuously aboard, and now, with the reissuing of this book, visitors may carry away the hard-won learning of one of the world's great sailormen.

Thanks to Exy's binding influence, the *Peking* veterans met from time to time in the US, where at least two shipmates of the 1929-30 voyage, besides Irving and Charles, ended up making their homes.

Irving, I know, had great affection and respect for these *Peking* veterans. I believe he came to see the ship as a paradigm of the Earth, sailing through the sea of space. I believe that his and Exy's vision of humanity bound on a common voyage, both in freedom and in service to a common cause, is one of the better visions of how we, the human race may learn to live together on this planet.

PETER STANFORD, 1995

APPENDIX

THE LIFE AND REBIRTH OF THE *PEKING*

NOTE: *This summary of the ship's career is expanded from an account first published in the* South Street Reporter, *journal of the South Street Seaport Museum in New York.*

During the last years of the sailing ship era, no German shipowners enjoyed greater fame and greater prestige than the F. Laeisz Company of Hamburg. Sailor-author Alan Villiers sums up their major accomplishment in this way: "Long after other owners gave up the deepsea sailing ship as doomed, [F. Laeisz] showed that such vessels, if properly conducted and well sailed, could still do their share of the world's work splendidly."

F. Laeisz built the last major merchant square rigger launched anywhere in the world, the four-masted *Padua* of 1926. The company still had two sailing ships in service in 1939, at the outbreak of World War II. And they were the owners of what has been called "the greatest sailing ship ever built," the mighty *Preussen* of 1902—the only sailing vessel to be square-rigged on five masts. But, as Villiers suggests, their fame had an even firmer basis. They had ships built of the highest quality, managed them efficiently, and got outstanding performances out of them. The F. Laeisz record for consistently good Cape Horn passages is unequalled.

The *Peking* of 1911 was typical of the later ships built for F. Laeisz. Around the turn of the century, the company had adopted the four-masted bark as its standard rig. Author J. Ferrell Colton, in his preface to a history of F. Laeisz, suggests that construction of this class of vessel really reached its peak with this ship and her sister *Passat*, ". . . equalled only by G.J.H. Siemens & Co.'s *Hans* and *Kurt* (later *Moshulu*)."

Peking was built by Blohm and Voss of Hamburg, a firm that remains active today, still building and repairing sailing ships on occasion, though now these vessels are the square-rigged schoolships of various nations. Like *Moshulu*, *Peking* belonged to the final stage in the evolution of the square-rigged merchant vessel. She was steered from a raised deck amidships, beneath which were the accommodations for both officers and crew. Fore and aft catwalks connected this midship house with the raised foredeck and raised poop. As much gear as possible was placed on these upper decks, to keep the men up off the main deck, which would be swept by heavy seas almost constantly off Cape Horn. Modern fittings included brace and halyard winches and mast tracks for the lighter yards.

F. Laeisz had been specialists in the trade between Europe and the west coast of South America since the 1860s. It was for this service that *Peking* was built. She was designed to carry cargoes of general merchandise around Cape Horn to Chile, generally to Talcahuano or Valparaiso, and return to Europe with bulk cargoes of nitrate from northern Chilean ports such as Iquique and Arica.

Command of *Peking* was given to Captain J. Hinrich Nissen, former master of the *Preussen*, which had been lost by collision November 7, 1910, when a steamer in the English Channel grossly underestimated her speed and failed to yield the right of way. Nissen commanded *Peking* for Laeisz until his retirement in 1926.

When World War I broke out in August 1914, *Peking* was caught at Valparaiso with five other ships of the company. She remained there the four years of the war and three years of treaty negotiations which followed. The exposed anchorage of Valparaiso is periodically swept by severe northerly gales. During one storm, on July 12, 1919, *Peking*'s near sistership *Petschili* was torn from her moorings and driven ashore, a total loss.

The Treaty of Versailles took away all Germany's ships above a certain tonnage. In 1921, the sailing ships laid up at Valparaiso were distributed among the various Allied countries. *Peking* went to the Italians. She made one passage, home to Europe, and was laid up again at Antwerp.

By this time F. Laeisz were re-establishing their fleet of sailing ships. In 1920 they completed the four-masted bark *Priwall*, whose construction had been suspended during the war, and in December 1921 they bought back *Peking*'s sister *Passat* for £13,000. The only other shipowner seeking to build a fleet of deepsea square riggers was Gustav Erikson of Finland. In 1922 he attempted to purchase *Peking* for £4,000. The following year he raised his bid to £9,000, but F. Laeisz had already bought her back for £8,500.

Peking returned to the nitrate trade. In 1926 she was altered to provide additional accommodations for cadets in training to become officers in the German merchant marine. Germany, like many northern European countries at that time, still required square-rig experience for licenses of deck officers in steam vessels. The fees paid to shipowners for carrying these cadets were a welcome extra source of income in the struggle to keep sailing ships in operation.

In the case of F. Laeisz, however, the death blow for their sailing-ship fleet was now developing; the price of nitrate was falling, because of the increased use of synthetic fertilizers. By 1931, things had become so bad that Laeisz took all their ships off the Chilean run, sent the two newest ships, *Priwall* and *Padua*, to Australia for grain cargoes, and put the remaining ships up for sale. *Peking*'s sistership *Passat*, and near sistership *Pamir*, were sold to Erikson. *Peking* herself was bought in September 1932 by the British Shaftesbury Homes and Arethusa Training Ship.

Since the mid-1800s, the British had been operating maritime-related schools of all types, both public and private, on board stationary hulks in various harbors and estuaries. Most of these hulks were obsolete wooden-hulled sailing warships. By the 1930s these ships were reaching the end of their days. It was to replace such a ship, the former HMS *Arethusa*, in use since 1874, that the Shaftesbury Homes acquired *Peking*.

The organization had been founded in 1843 as the National Refuges for Homeless and Destitute Children. Twenty years later its president, the Seventh Earl of Shaftesbury, proposed the introduction of a maritime curriculum and use of a training hulk. The Admiralty soon provided the first ship for the school, the frigate HMS *Chichester*, and she in turn was replaced by the larger HMS *Arethusa*, a 50-gun vessel built in 1849.

The old *Arethusa* had lain at Greenhithe on the Thames, near London, but by 1932 the school was re-located on the Medway River at the village of Upnor. Facilities fitted in *Peking* for her new career included berthing space, classrooms, offices, a gymnasium and assembly hall, a branch of the County library, and a chapel. Her lighter yards were removed and given to the stationary training ship *Worcester* at Greenhithe.

The rebuilt *Peking* was formally opened as a school-ship at ceremonies on July 25, 1933, and re-christened *Arethusa*. Seven years later, with the war in progress, the school moved to Salcombe, Devonshire, in the west of England, and the ship was loaned to the Royal Navy for use as accommodations for engineering petty offic-ers at the Chatham Dockyard. Since there was already an HMS *Arethusa*, a light cruiser, the old ship was tem-porarily renamed HMS *Peking*.

After the war she returned to her duties as a school-ship. But over the years upkeep became more and more expensive. Her rig was reduced rather than renewed. First all yards were removed from main and mizzen masts, giving her the appearance of a barkentine. Then, only a few years later, the three topgallant masts were cut off and the number of yards on the foremast was reduced to two. By 1974 it was decided to sell the ship and move the school ashore.

Arethusa was advertised for sale and, on October 31, 1974 at public auction, was purchased by the J. Aron Charitable Foundation of New York for the South Street Seaport Museum, for the sum of £70,000. At the last moment, there was some interest in keeping the ship in England, and in making her a museum ship at Hamburg, but pledges of financial support fell far short of the final price in both cases. In compliance with the wishes of the Shaftesbury Homes, the ship was given back her original name.

A "joint venture" committee, composed of trustees of the South Street Seaport Museum and representatives of the J. Aron Charitable Foundation, was formed to oversee getting the *Peking* to New York and the first phases of her restoration. On January 1, 1975, this committee appointed Commander H.A. Paulsen (USCG ret.), one-time captain of the training bark *Eagle*, to supervise the actual work. *Peking* left her berth in the Medway River on March 6, 1975 and entered a drydock at Blackwall on the Thames east of London on March 10th.

on March 10th.

The work done at Blackwall was mainly limited to that necessary to make the vessel seaworthy for the tow to New York. Eighteen badly wasted plates in the waterline area were replaced. The new plates were rivetted in place, as the originals had been 64 years before. "Rivetting was done not only to match the original construction," Cdr. Paulsen reported, "but also to eliminate the stiffness that welding would bring to the hull, with the associated problems of cracks forming in the welded area. The shipyard had difficulty in finding sufficient trained men to install over 12,000 rivets," he continued. "But eventually five teams of five men were assembled. And the capable men found to do the riveting were a shot in the arm for all the middle-aged men of the world—every team member had more than four decades behind him!"

Various openings in the ship's sides made by the school were sealed up, including 125 portholes in the tweendeck and lower hold areas. The hull was cleaned and painted from the waterline down. The hatches were securely sealed. The two surviving yards on the foremast were sent down and stowed on deck, the fore lower yard just fitting into the after well deck with inches to spare. And the carved wooden shield and scrollwork decoration was removed from the bow and stowed in the midship house.

Peking left England on July 5, 1975, in tow of the

ful, aside from some wide course changes to avoid storms, and one anxious moment when *Peking* threatened to run down the tug, which had stopped for engine repairs. On July 22, seventeen days out, *Peking* was towed under the Verrazzano Bridge and turned over to harbor tugs which berthed her at the Pouch Terminal in Staten Island. One month later she was shifted to the Brewer Drydock Co. shipyard, also on Staten Island, to begin the first phase of restoration.

Several structures erected on deck when the ship was a school were removed, including water tanks on the foredeck, midship deck and poop; and a large steel deckhouse in the forward well deck which had contained a galley and bakery. The hull was sandblasted above the waterline, including inside the bulwarks, and a return was made to the original F. Laeisz color scheme in all areas. The bow emblem, painted white when she was a school, was sent away to be restored and repainted in white, green, and gold, with red letters "FL" again in place on the shield. Finally, the two surviving yards were once again crossed on the foremast. On November 22, 1975, with the traditional New York fireboat welcome, *Peking* was towed through the harbor to her new home at the Seaport's Pier 16 on the East River below the Brooklyn Bridge.

During the spring of 1976, the focus of restoration work shifted to getting a full complement of yards aloft by that July, and installing an exhibit in parts of the by that July, and installing an exhibit in parts of the midship house which had been totally altered when she was a school. This exhibit, a collection of photographs of the ship and vessels of her type arranged to tell her history and something about life on board, opened in time for July 4th, when the Seaport was host to several of the visiting schoolships taking part in Operation Sail 1976. By this time *Peking* had been fitted with new topgallant masts, and crossed all but the three royal yards, the new spars having been fabricated by a firm on Long Island.

The *Peking* at the South Street Seaport Museum

Since July 1976, the remaining yards have been crossed and all spars rigged with lifts and braces. Remaining school structures built into the break of the foredeck have been removed. Two original spaces in the midship house, the starboard forecastle and the space for storing and working on sails, have been partially restored and outfitted. Research is now underway for a partial restoration of the original officers' accommodations.

Work on *Peking* parallels similar restoration of the 1885 British full-rigged ship *Wavertree*, lying at the Museum's Pier 15, looking toward the day when the Seaport will have two majestic square-rigged vessels in a partial re-creation of the South Street of the 1800s when bowsprits arched over the roadway from the Battery northward as far as the eye could see.

NORMAN J. BROUWER
Ship Historian
South Street Seaport Museum

SEA HISTORY PRESS

Sea History Press is the publishing arm of the National Maritime Historical Society, an educational institution founded in 1963 and dedicated to the challenging heritage of American seafaring. Members receive the quarterly magazine *Sea History*. Their membership helps keep that vital heritage in life. For membership information, write NMHS, 5 John Walsh Boulevard, Peekskill NY 10566.

IRVING & EXY JOHNSON FUND

In keeping with the educational mission of the National Maritime Historical Society, part of the proceeds from the sale of *The Peking Battles Cape Horn* will go to an Irving & Exy Johnson Fund to help more young people go to sea under sail, and part will go to support the *Peking* herself at the South Street Seaport Museum in New York City.